**PRACTICE
MAKES
PERFECT**

German
Pronouns
and
Prepositions

**PRACTICE
MAKES
PERFECT**

German
Pronouns
and
Prepositions

Second Edition

Ed Swick

New York   Chicago   San Francisco   Lisbon   London   Madrid   Mexico City
Milan   New Delhi   San Juan   Seoul   Singapore   Sydney   Toronto

Contents

APPENDIXES   **169**

Introduction

Pronouns and prepositions are often undervalued and considered insignificant aspects of language study. They are even sometimes entirely overlooked. But pronouns and prepositions—whether English or German—play an important role in language. In fact, many people study German for years and become masters of conjugations and declensions but continue to have only a basic grasp of the many uses of pronouns and prepositions.

This book will help to overcome this neglectful attitude. It puts pronouns and prepositions under a bright light to illuminate their importance in language learning and to provide you with new insight into their mechanics. You will find detailed explanations of their functions and numerous examples to add clarity to those functions.

You will also find an abundance of exercises for practicing the new concepts you learn. The exercises appear in different formats in order to give you practice with pronouns and prepositions *from different angles*. Some of the exercises ask you to select the word that completes a sentence correctly. Others ask you to complete a sentence with any appropriate word or phrase of your choosing. Still others ask you to write an original sentence that includes a specific phrase. There is an Answer Key at the back of the book so that you can track your progress.

Knowing how to identify pronouns and prepositions is only part of the story. Knowing how they *function* is also necessary. Knowing *where* and *when* pronouns and prepositions are used is another key to unlocking their secrets. It is important to have the *whole story*, because pronouns and prepositions are more than just little words that adorn sentences. They help to make sentences flow and to sound interesting and meaningful. This book will guide you through the *whole story*.

Take advantage of the contents of this book and increase your ability to use pronouns and prepositions effectively and accurately. This is an opportunity to bring your German skills to a higher level.

PART I

PRONOUNS

You already know that *pronouns replace nouns* in a sentence, and you are certainly familiar with the personal pronouns in German: **ich**, **du**, **er**, **sie**, **es**, **wir**, **ihr**, and **Sie**. But the story about pronouns continues beyond the personal pronouns.

For one thing, the variety of pronouns in German is rather large. They range from personal pronouns, which everyone identifies with ease, to possessive pronouns, demonstrative pronouns, relative pronouns, reflexive pronouns, reciprocal pronouns, and others. These types of pronouns may be unfamiliar to you now, but once you have experience with these pronouns and adequate practice, they will make sense to you, and you will gain the skill to use pronouns more effectively.

In this section of the book, you will be introduced to the various types of German pronouns. They will be described for you, and they will be illustrated with examples. Then you will have the opportunity to practice with them in a variety of exercises.

As a result, you will have developed a better understanding of these pronouns and will have increased your effectiveness in using them. Using pronouns well will allow you to streamline your speech and writing and to make your use of German more effective.

Pronouns in the Nominative Case

The English personal pronouns used as the subject of a sentence are equivalent to the German nominative case pronouns, which are used as the subject of a German sentence.

English pronouns	German pronouns
I	ich
you	du, ihr, Sie
he	er
she	sie
it	es
we	wir
they	sie

The following examples show pronouns used as the subject of a sentence.

> **Ich** wohne in Bonn.
> *I live in Bonn.*

> **Sie** ist meine Schwester.
> *She is my sister.*

> Wo sind **wir**?
> *Where are we?*

The German pronouns are used in much the same way as the English pronouns, with the important exception of the pronouns that mean *you* (**du**, **ihr**, and **Sie**).

Use **du** when speaking to a small child, a family member, or a close friend.

> Wie alt bist **du** jetzt, Franz? Sieben oder acht?
> *How old are you now, Franz? Seven or eight?*

Use **ihr** when speaking to more than one child, family member, or close friend.

> Erik! Gudrun! Kinder! Wo seid **ihr**?
> *Erik! Gudrun! Children! Where are you?*

Use **Sie** when speaking to adults who are unfamiliar, as well as to people with whom you regularly deal on a formal basis (for example, your boss, your professor, your physician, and the local shopkeeper).

> Können **Sie** mir sagen bitte, wo das Thaliatheater ist? (*to a stranger on the street*)
> *Can you please tell me where the Thalia Theater is?*

> Sind **Sie** heute beschäftigt, Herr Doktor?
> *Are you busy today, Doctor?*

These differences can be generalized in the following chart.

du   a singular informal pronoun
ihr   a plural informal pronoun (the plural of **du**)
Sie   a singular or plural formal pronoun

The pronoun **sie** may sometimes seem confusing, because it can mean *she, they,* or (when capitalized—**Sie**) *you*. But Germans have no difficulty in distinguishing the meaning of this pronoun: The context of a conversation or of a written or printed text clearly indicates the intended meaning of **sie**.

> „Kennst du diese Frau?" „Ja, **sie** ist meine Mutter."
> *"Do you know this woman?" "Yes, she's my mother."*

> „Kennst du diese Mädchen?" „Ja, **sie** sind meine Schwestern."
> *"Do you know these girls?" "Yes, they're my sisters."*

> „Sind **Sie** Deutscher?" „Nein, ich bin Schweizer."
> *"Are you German?" "No, I'm Swiss."*

In addition, when **sie** means *she,* the verb is singular. When **sie** means *they,* the verb is plural.

> **Sie** ist in Berlin.
> *She is in Berlin.*

> **Sie** sind in Berlin.
> *They are in Berlin.*

German has two additional nominative case pronouns: **wer** and **was**. These are interrogative pronouns and ask the question *who* or *what*.

> **Wer** ist das?
> *Who's that?*

> **Was** liegt auf dem Boden?
> *What's lying on the floor?*

When changing a nominative case noun to a nominative case pronoun, the pronoun must have the same gender and number as the noun. Masculine nouns change to **er**, feminine nouns change to **sie**, and neuter nouns change to **es**. All plural nouns become **sie**.

> **Der Lehrer** ist zu Hause.
> *The teacher is at home.*
> **Er** ist zu Hause.
> *He is at home.*

Die Lehrerin ist zu Hause.
The teacher is at home.
Sie ist zu Hause.
She is at home.

Das Haus ist alt.
The house is old.
Es ist alt.
It's old.

Die Häuser sind alt.
The houses are old.
Sie sind alt.
They are old.

Übung 1-1

Rewrite each sentence, changing the word or phrase in boldface to the appropriate pronoun.

1. **Das Kind** hat lange geschlafen.

   _____

2. Ist **die alte Frau** deine Großmutter?

   _____

3. **Herr Keller** hat sich gestern das Bein gebrochen.

   _____

4. **Viele Leute** kämpfen gegen das Schicksal.

   _____

5. Wo sind **die Stühle**?

   _____

6. **Sabine** wird den Ofen heizen.

   _____

7. **Die junge Ärztin** war mit dieser Arbeit zufrieden.

   _____

8. **Die Tiere und Pflanzen einer tropischen Insel** wachsen nicht hier.

   _____

9. Hat **Karl** meinen Pullover genommen?

_____

10. **Das nette Mädchen** wohnt nicht weit von uns.

_____

Each nominative case pronoun requires the use of a specific verb form. The following chart presents several verb types in the present tense and the form required for each pronoun.

	Regular verb	Irregular verb	**haben**	**sein**	Modal
ich	sage	lese	habe	bin	kann
du	sagst	liest	hast	bist	kannst
er	sagt	liest	hat	ist	kann
sie	sagt	liest	hat	ist	kann
es	sagt	liest	hat	ist	kann
wir	sagen	lesen	haben	sind	können
ihr	sagt	lest	habt	seid	könnt
sie	sagen	lesen	haben	sind	können
Sie	sagen	lesen	haben	sind	können

The forms for the past tense of these verbs follow.

	Regular verb	Irregular verb	**haben**	**sein**	Modal
ich	sagte	las	hatte	war	konnte
du	sagtest	lasest	hattest	warst	konntest
er	sagte	las	hatte	war	konnte
sie	sagte	las	hatte	war	konnte
es	sagte	las	hatte	war	konnte
wir	sagten	lasen	hatten	waren	konnten
ihr	sagtet	last	hattet	wart	konntet
sie	sagten	lasen	hatten	waren	konnten
Sie	sagten	lasen	hatten	waren	konnten

The interrogative pronouns **wer** and **was** use a third-person singular (**er**, **sie**, **es**) form of the verb.

The pronoun **es** is used in many _impersonal expressions,_ which require a subject to make the sentence complete but which do not specify who or what is carrying out the action of the verb. The action is performed by an _impersonal it_. This kind of expression also occurs in English.

> **Es** regnet.
> _It's raining._ (What's raining? It!)

> **Es** ist kalt.
> _It's cold._

> **Es** wird schon dunkel.
> _It's already getting dark._

The English verb *to get* has numerous meanings and uses. For a complete overview of this verb and its possible German translations, see Appendix A.

Übung	1-2

Rewrite each sentence in the present tense, substituting the pronouns **ich**, **du**, **wir**, *and* **ihr** *for the third-person subject in the original.*

1. Er begeht ein Verbrechen.

   a. Ich _____.

   b. Du _____.

   c. Wir _____.

   d. Ihr _____.

2. Sie ist fertig zur Reise.

   a. Ich _____.

   b. Du _____.

   c. Wir _____.

   d. Ihr _____.

3. Sie borgen dem Kaufmann Geld.

   a. Ich _____.

   b. Du _____.

   c. Wir _____.

   d. Ihr _____.

4. Herr Schneider hat die Fragen beantwortet.

   a. Ich _____.

   b. Du _____.

   c. Wir _____.

   d. Ihr _____.

Übung   1-3

Rewrite each sentence in the past tense, substituting the pronouns **ich**, **du**, **wir**, *and* **ihr** *for the third-person subject in the original.*

1. Die Lehrerin brachte die Bücher mit.

    a. Ich _____.

    b. Du _____.

    c. Wir _____.

    d. Ihr _____.

2. Er wollte zu Hause bleiben.

    a. Ich _____.

    b. Du _____.

    c. Wir _____.

    d. Ihr _____.

3. Sie kaufte ein Haus in Freiburg.

    a. Ich _____.

    b. Du _____.

    c. Wir _____.

    d. Ihr _____.

Übung   1-4

Rewrite each sentence, changing the pronoun in boldface to any appropriate noun or phrase.

1. **Er** ist ein Freund von mir.

    _____

2. **Sie** hat ihre Tasche wieder verloren.

    _____

3. **Es** schläft auf dem Sofa.

    _____

4. **Wir** denken oft an euch.

_____

5. Sind **sie** noch in der Hauptstadt?

_____

Übung   1-5

Rewrite each sentence as a question, replacing the word or phrase in boldface with either **wer** _or_ **was**.

EXAMPLE   **Karl** wohnt in Stuttgart.

_____ _Wer wohnt in Stuttgart?_ _____

1. **Es** kostet nur zehn Euro.

_____

2. **Die kleinsten Kinder** müssen sofort nach Hause gehen.

_____

3. **Sie** ist eine Nonne.

_____

4. **Der neue Fernsehapparat** ist kaputt.

_____

5. **Mein Neffe** arbeitet als Juwelier.

_____

Übung   1-6

Circle the word or phrase in boldface that is an appropriate subject for each sentence. In this exercise, **Sie** _(sing.) and_ **Sie** _(pl.) represent third-person pronouns._

1. **Ich** | **Du** | **Meine Kusinen** bin wieder krank geworden.

2. **Er** | **Wir** | **Ein neuer Gast** haben Onkel Heinrich besucht.

3. **Sie** (_sing._) | **Sie** (_pl._) | **Karl** verstehen das nicht.

4. **Es** | **Ihr** | **Diese Mädchen** ist ziemlich kalt.

5. Geht **Sie** (_pl._) | **ihr** | **du** wieder aufs Land?

6. **Ich** | **Er** | **Deine Kinder** lässt uns im Stich.

7. **Wir** | **Sie** *(sing.)* | **Die Soldaten** hilft ihren Eltern.

8. **Ihr** | **Sie** *(pl.)* | **Gudrun** habt eine großen Storch gesehen.

9. Hört **du** | **sie** *(pl.)* | **Erhardt** die Musik?

10. **Sie** *(sing.)* | **Wir** | **Ich** können ein paar Sätze schreiben.

11. **Es** | **Sie** *(pl.)* | **Wer** mag sein.

12. **Du** | **Wir** | **Mein Vetter** kann Spanisch und Russisch.

13. Warum warst **Sie** *(pl.)* | **ihr** | **du** im Krankenhaus?

14. **Sie** *(pl.)* | **Wir** | **Das Schauspiel** war nicht so gut, wie wir erwartet hatten.

15. **Ich** | **Du** | **Ihre Geschwister** habe gehorchen müssen.

Pronouns and Gender

The concept of gender is not identical in English and German. English gender is primarily *sexual* gender. English speakers think of males as the masculine gender, females as the feminine gender, and inanimate objects as the neuter gender. When any of these is made plural, gender disappears and all plural people and things are just *plural*.

The concept of gender in German differs from that in English. Most German nouns referring to males are the masculine gender and can be replaced by the masculine pronoun **er**. The definite article in the nominative case of these nouns is always **der**, and the indefinite article in the nominative case is **ein**.

der Mann	*the man*	**er**
der Lehrer	*the (male) teacher*	**er**
der Bruder	*the brother*	**er**

In German, most nouns referring to females are the feminine gender and can be replaced by the feminine pronoun **sie**. The definite article in the nominative case of these nouns is always **die**, and the indefinite article in the nominative case is **eine**.

die Frau	*the woman*	**sie**
die Lehrerin	*the (female) teacher*	**sie**
die Tochter	*the daughter*	**sie**

At this point, German and English part ways and German uses another concept for gender. The formation of a noun can determine its gender—not just the sex of a person. For example, words that end in **-er**, **-en**, or **-el** tend to be masculine, even if they are inanimate objects.

Animate noun		Pronoun
der Vater	*the father*	**er**
der Onkel	*the uncle*	**er**
der Vetter	*the (male) cousin*	**er**

Inanimate noun		Pronoun
der Körper	*the body*	**er**
der Mantel	*the coat*	**er**
der Wagen	*the car*	**er**

11

English speakers substitute the pronoun *it* for nouns like *body, coat,* and *car.* In German, however, those words are masculine. German speakers are not calling such inanimate objects *he*; they are simply identifying them as *masculine.*

The same is true for feminine nouns. Some can identify animate objects, and others can identify inanimate ones.

Animate noun		Pronoun
die Mutter	*the mother*	**sie**
die Tante	*the aunt*	**sie**
die Dame	*the lady*	**sie**

Inanimate noun		Pronoun
die Zeit	*the time*	**sie**
die Lampe	*the lamp*	**sie**
die Prüfung	*the test*	**sie**

German speakers are not calling a lamp *she*; they are simply identifying it as *feminine.*

Although neuter nouns in English are inanimate objects, in German they can also be persons or animals, because the gender of a German noun is determined by how the noun is formed or by a long tradition of being associated with a certain gender. The definite article in the nominative case of neuter nouns is always **das**, and their indefinite article in the nominative case is **ein**. The following chart gives examples of animate and inanimate neuter nouns.

Animate noun		Pronoun
das Pferd	*the horse*	**es**
das Kind	*the child*	**es**
das Mädchen	*the girl*	**es**

Inanimate noun		Pronoun
das Haus	*the house*	**es**
das Bild	*the picture*	**es**
das Geld	*the money*	**es**

Many German nouns that are diminutives end in **-chen** or **-lein**, and all such nouns are neuter. That's why **das Mädchen** (*the girl*) and **das Fräulein** (*the young woman*) are neuter and are replaced by the neuter pronoun **es**. By using the pronoun **es**, German speakers are not calling a girl or a young woman *it*; they are simply conforming to the gender of the German noun.

This concept of gender in German disappears when nouns and pronouns become plural. The definite article in the nominative case for plural nouns is always **die**. All plural nouns in the nominative case are replaced by the plural pronoun **sie**.

der Mann	*the man*	**er**	die Männer	*the men*	**sie**
die Frau	*the woman*	**sie**	die Frauen	*the women*	**sie**
das Kind	*the child*	**es**	die Kinder	*the children*	**sie**
der Wagen	*the car*	**er**	die Wagen	*the cars*	**sie**
die Lampe	*the lamp*	**sie**	die Lampen	*the lamps*	**sie**
das Haus	*the house*	**es**	die Häuser	*the houses*	**sie**

Übung	**2-1**

*Write the English translation of the German noun in the first blank. In the second blank, write the appropriate pronoun replacement for the German noun (**er**, **sie** (sing.), **es**, *or* **sie** (pl.)).*

1. Stuhl _____ _____

2. Kreide _____ _____

3. Geld _____ _____

4. Zeitungen _____ _____

5. Leute _____ _____

6. Gast _____ _____

7. Freundin _____ _____

8. Fräulein _____ _____

9. Sportler _____ _____

10. Rennwagen _____ _____

Übung	**2-2**

Rewrite each sentence, changing the word or phrase in boldface to the appropriate pronoun.

1. **Das Kino** ist ziemlich weit von hier.

    _____

2. Wo ist **das Mädchen von Griechenland**?

    _____

3. **Eine schöne Wohnung** ist nur noch ein Traum.

    _____

4. **Die alte Katze** ist sehr krank geworden.

    _____

5. Kann **Helmut** Klavier spielen?

    _____

6. **Der Hut** war schmutzig.

_____

7. **Meine Freunde** kommen aus England.

_____

8. Warum sitzen **dein Vater und deine Mutter** in der Küche?

_____

9. **Ein neuer Tisch** stand in der Mitte des Zimmers.

_____

10. **Die Klapperschlange** sieht tot aus.

_____

There is no indefinite article for plural nouns in German. Instead, a plural noun can stand alone to identify its *indefinite* meaning.

Plural with the definite article
_____

die Leute	*the people* (specific ones)
die Häuser	*the houses*
die Zeitungen	*the newspapers*

Plural with indefinite meaning
_____

Leute	*people* (in general)
Häuser	*houses*
Zeitungen	*newspapers*

Whether a plural noun is definite or indefinite, it is always replaced by the plural form of the pronoun, **sie**.

Übung   2-3

Circle the noun or phrase that is the appropriate replacement for the subject pronoun in each sentence.

1. Er kommt aus Spanien.   Die Menschen | Unser Gast | Karin und Helga

2. Sind sie in diesem Schrank?   die Bücher | die Zeitschrift | die Katze

3. Ist er neu?   der Wagen | dein Fahrrad | ihre Bluse

4. Es ist wieder krank geworden.   Luise | Meine Freunde | Das Kind

5. Sie ist wirklich sehr schön.   Die Musik | Ein Klavier | Sein Radio

6. Sie arbeiten in einer Fabrik.   Meine Eltern | Die Hose | Eine Schlange

  7. Es ist unter dem Tisch.   Eine Tasse | Teller | Das Glas

  8. Er ist ziemlich weit von hier.   Ein Hotel | Der Berg | Die Alpen

  9. Ist sie eine Freundin von euch?   Angelika | die Wandtafel | eine Armbanduhr

 10. Sie durften es nicht tun.   Unser Professor | Diese Diplomaten | Ein Mädchen

 11. Morgen geht er wieder aufs Land.   sein Onkel | die Touristen | der Handschuh

 12. War es in der Schublade?   jene Mäntel | das Messer | mein neuer Wagen

 13. Auf dem Dach sieht sie es.   Frau Bauer | Herr Bauer | die Bauern

 14. Er wird mit dem Auto nach Wien fahren.   Ein Zug | Ihr Vetter | Seine Schwestern

 15. Sie lernen schnell.   Die Musik | Diese Studentin | Ihre Kinder

Pronouns in the Accusative Case

When an English noun is made the direct object in a sentence, it does not change—it looks like it does when it is the subject of a sentence. Most English pronouns, however, change when used as a direct object.

Subject	Direct object
*The **boy** is ten years old.*	*Do you know the **boy**?*
***He** is ten years old.*	*Do you know **him**?*
*The **woman** is quite young.*	*Do you know the **woman**?*
***She** is quite young.*	*Do you know **her**?*

The following chart gives the subject and direct object forms of the personal pronoun in English.

Subject pronouns	Direct object pronouns
I	*me*
you	*you*
he	*him*
she	*her*
it	*it*
we	*us*
they	*them*

German treats nouns somewhat differently. Masculine singular nouns require a new form of the article when used as a direct object. Feminine, neuter, and plural nouns do not change their article when used as direct objects. German direct objects are expressed in the accusative case.

Nominative nouns	Accusative nouns	
der Laden	den Laden	*the store*
die Kreide	die Kreide	*the chalk*
das Flugzeug	das Flugzeug	*the airplane*
die Leute	die Leute	*the people*

Most German pronouns have a different form when used as direct objects in the accusative case. The only exceptions are **sie** (*sing.*), **es**, **sie** (*pl.*), and **was**.

Nominative pronouns	Accusative pronouns
ich	mich
du	dich
er	ihn
sie (*sing.*)	sie
es	es
wir	uns
ihr	euch
sie (*pl.*)	sie
Sie	Sie
wer	wen
was	was

To use the accusative pronouns correctly, you must know how to identify a direct object. In English, you ask *whom* or *what* of the verb; the answer is the direct object.

John kissed Mary.	*Whom did he kiss?*	***Mary*** = direct object
I bought a new car.	*What did I buy?*	***a new car*** = direct object

The same test can be used in German. You ask **wen** or **was** of the verb; the answer is the direct object.

Hans küsste Maria.	Wen küsste Hans?	**Maria** = direct object (accusative case)
Ich kaufte einen neuen Wagen.	Was kaufte ich?	**einen neuen Wagen** = direct object (accusative case)

Pronouns substituted for direct object nouns must be accusative case pronouns.

„Hans küsste Maria." „Wirklich? Hans küsste **sie**?"
"Hans kissed Maria." "Really? Hans kissed her?"

„Ich kaufte einen neuen Wagen." „Wirklich? Du kauftest **ihn**?"
"I bought a new car." "Really? You bought it?"

Notice that the pronouns substituted in these examples are the same gender and number as the nouns they replace and are, of course, in the accusative case: **Maria** → **sie** and **einen neuen Wagen** → **ihn**.

The following examples show each of the accusative case pronouns in German used as a direct object in complete sentences.

ich	Der Tiger hat **mich** angegriffen.	*The tiger attacked me.*
du	Sie kennen **dich** nicht.	*They don't know you.*
er	Sie hat **ihn** nie geliebt.	*She never loved him.*
sie	Jede Woche besuche ich **sie**.	*I visit her every week.*
es	Er versteht **es** nicht.	*He doesn't understand it.*
wir	Karin hat **uns** eingeladen.	*Karin invited us.*
ihr	Er wird **euch** nie vergessen.	*He will never forget you.*
sie	Ich kann **sie** nicht sehen.	*I can't see them.*
Sie	Ich werde **Sie** vorstellen.	*I'll introduce you.*
wer	**Wen** hast du besucht?	*Whom did you visit?*
was	**Was** haben Sie gekauft?	*What did you buy?*

Übung   3-1

Rewrite each sentence, changing the word or phrase in boldface to the appropriate pronoun.

1. Im Sommer werden wir **unsere Verwandten in New York** besuchen.

   _____

2. Ich kenne **das Mädchen** nicht.

   _____

3. Gudrun hat **die Fragen** zu langsam beantwortet.

   _____

4. Kannst du **ihre Handschrift** lesen?

   _____

5. Wir haben **den Zug** verpasst!

   _____

6. Wer kann **dieses Problem** lösen?

   _____

7. Mutter hat **meinen Regenmantel** im Keller gefunden.

   _____

8. Der Blitz hat **zwei Pferde** getötet.

   _____

9. Martin wird **eine weiße Nelke** kaufen.

   _____

10. Ich liebe **das schöne Wetter.**

   _____

In rare instances, there can be two accusative objects in the same sentence.

> Frau Schuhmann hat **die Kinder** (1) **die neue Rechtschreibung** (2) gelehrt.
> *Mrs. Schuhmann taught the children the new orthography.*

> Sie nannte **den Dieb** (1) **einen Lügner** (2).
> *She called the thief a liar.*

If pronouns replace accusative nouns, they must, of course, be accusative case pronouns.

> Frau Schuhmann hat **sie** die neue Rechtschreibung gelehrt.
> *Mrs. Schuhmann taught them the new orthography.*

Sie nannte **ihn** einen Lügner.
She called him a liar.

Sentences with two accusative objects tend to occur with only a few verbs: **heißen**, **kosten**, **lehren**, **nennen**, **rufen**, **schelten**, **schimpfen**, and **taufen**.

When substituting a pronoun for an accusative noun, you must be aware of not only the proper case for the pronoun but also its gender. The English inanimate pronoun is always *it,* but German inanimate nouns can be masculine, feminine, or neuter. Therefore, the accusative form of the pronoun must be the same gender as the noun in the accusative case.

„Verstehst du **diesen Satz**?“ „Nein, ich verstehe **ihn** nicht.“
"Do you understand this sentence?" "No, I don't understand it."

„Verstehst du **diese Oper**?“ „Nein, ich verstehe **sie** nicht.“
"Do you understand this opera?" "No, I don't understand it."

„Verstehst du **dieses Problem**?“ „Nein, ich verstehe **es** nicht.“
"Do you understand this problem?" "No, I don't understand it."

„Verstehst du **diese Sätze**?“ „Nein, ich verstehe **sie** nicht.“
"Do you understand these sentences?" "No, I don't understand them."

It is only with animate nouns that German and English replace nouns with pronouns in a similar way.

„Kennst du **diesen Mann**?“ „Nein, ich kenne **ihn** nicht.“
"Do you know this man?" "No, I don't know him."

„Kennst du **diese Dame**?“ „Nein, ich kenne **sie** nicht.“
"Do you know this lady?" "No, I don't know her."

„Kennst du **dieses Kind**?“ „Nein, ich kenne **es** nicht.“
"Do you know this child?" "No, I don't know him/her."

„Kennst du **diese Leute**?“ „Nein, ich kenne **sie** nicht.“
"Do you know these people?" "No, I don't know them."

Übung	3-2

Rewrite each sentence, changing the accusative case pronoun to any appropriate noun.

1. Ich habe ihn in Kanada kennen gelernt.

   _____

2. Wo hast du es gefunden?

   _____

3. Er hat sie auf dem Tisch stehen gelassen.

   _____

4. Onkel Karl hat ihn versteckt.

   _____

5. Wirst du uns besuchen?

_____

6. Man baut sie am Rande des Waldes.

_____

7. Tante Luise hat es auf das Bett gelegt.

_____

Note: When changing a noun phrase that includes **ich** to a pronoun, you must use a form of **wir**.

> **Karl und ich** warten noch.
> _Karl and I are still waiting._
> **Wir** warten noch.
> _We're still waiting._
>
> Sie kennen **Karl und mich.**
> _They know Karl and me._
> Sie kennen **uns.**
> _They know us._

As shown in these examples, this substitution can be used for a nominative subject (**Karl und ich** = **wir**) and for an accusative direct object (**Karl und mich** = **uns**).

Übung	3-3

Rewrite each sentence as a question, replacing the noun or pronoun in boldface with either **wer** or **was**.

EXAMPLE   Er hat **es** gefunden.

_____ _Was hat er gefunden?_ _____

1. Ich werde **meinen Urlaub** in Innsbruck verleben.

_____

2. Mein Vetter kennt **ihn** nicht.

_____

3. Martin kaufte **das Geschenk** für seine Schwester.

_____

4. Sie hat seit ihrer Jugend **Sport** getrieben.

_____

5. Der Arbeitslose verdient **nichts**.

_____

6. Wir treffen **sie** am Hauptbahnhof.

_____

7. Meine Tante hat **den Pförtner** gefragt.

_____

8. Ich liebe **meine Heimat** am meisten.

_____

9. Seine Eltern haben **Sie** im Kaufhaus gesehen.

_____

10. Solche Umstände ärgern **mich**.

_____

Übung   **3-4**

Circle the pronoun that best completes each sentence.

1. Ich habe _____ einfach vergessen.   mich | es | du

2. Sie sieht _____ auf dem Dach.   ihn | wir | ihr

3. Wir müssen _____ fragen.   sie | ihr | ich

4. Morgen kaufen wir _____.   uns | Sie | ihn

5. Die Kinder dürfen _____ nicht tun.   du | dich | es

6. Wo sind meine Schuhe? Hast du _____?   sie | es | ihn

7. Ich höre _____ singen.   er | euch | wir

8. Wir besuchen _____ im Krankenhaus.   ihr | ich | sie

9. Mögen Sie _____ nicht?   er | ich | ihn

10. Wir haben _____ verpasst!   ihn | mich | ihr

Pronouns in the Dative Case

English pronouns used as indirect objects are the same as the pronouns used as direct objects. In German, however, indirect objects are in the dative case, and German has dative case pronouns.

Nominative	Accusative	Dative
ich	mich	mir
du	dich	dir
er	ihn	ihm
sie	sie	ihr
es	es	ihm
wir	uns	uns
ihr	euch	euch
sie	sie	ihnen
Sie	Sie	Ihnen
wer	wen	wem
was	was	—

If a German noun is used as an indirect object, it must be in the dative case. When a pronoun replaces a dative case noun, it must be a dative case pronoun.

> Ich gebe **dem Kind** ein Glas Wasser.
> *I give the child a glass of water.*
> Ich gebe **ihm** ein Glas Wasser.
> *I give him a glass of water.*

> Wir zeigen es **den Touristen**.
> *We show it to the tourists.*
> Wir zeigen es **ihnen**.
> *We show it to them.*

Notice that, when the direct object is a pronoun, the English preposition *to* or *for* is used with a noun or pronoun that is the indirect object.

Direct object as noun	Direct object as pronoun
*I give the child **a glass of water**.*	*I give **it** to the child.*
*I give him **a glass of water**.*	*I give **it** to him.*

In German, however, the dative case for indirect objects is always used *without a preposition*.

Direct object as noun	Direct object as pronoun
Ich gebe dem Kind **ein Glas Wasser**.	Ich gebe **es** dem Kind.
Ich gebe ihm **ein Glas Wasser**.	Ich gebe **es** ihm.

It is important to know how to identify an indirect object in order to apply the dative case appropriately. In English, you ask *to whom* or *for whom* of the verb; the answer to the question is the indirect object.

I give you ten dollars.	*To whom do I give ten dollars?*	**you** = indirect object
We bought John a car.	*For whom did we buy a car?*	***John*** = indirect object

It works the same way in German. You ask **wem** of the verb; the answer is the indirect object.

Ich gebe **euch** zehn Euro. *I give you ten euros.*	Wem gebe ich zehn Euro?	**euch** = indirect object (dative case)
Wir kauften **Johann** einen Wagen. *We bought Johann a car.*	Wem kauften wir einen Wagen?	**Johann** = indirect object (dative case)

Notice that sentences that have an indirect object also have a direct object (accusative case). In the examples above, the direct objects are **zehn Euro** and **einen Wagen**.

The following examples show each of the dative case pronouns in German used as an indirect object in complete sentences. Pronouns that replace dative case nouns or that are in the indirect object position in a sentence are in the dative case.

> Onkel Peter hat **Karl** einen Brief geschrieben.
> *Uncle Peter has written Karl a letter.*

ich	Onkel Peter hat **mir** einen Brief geschrieben.
du	Onkel Peter hat **dir** einen Brief geschrieben.
er	Onkel Peter hat **ihm** einen Brief geschrieben.
sie	Onkel Peter hat **ihr** einen Brief geschrieben.
es	Onkel Peter hat **ihm** einen Brief geschrieben.
wir	Onkel Peter hat **uns** einen Brief geschrieben.
ihr	Onkel Peter hat **euch** einen Brief geschrieben.
sie	Onkel Peter hat **ihnen** einen Brief geschrieben.
Sie	Onkel Peter hat **Ihnen** einen Brief geschrieben.
wer	**Wem** hat Onkel Peter einen Brief geschrieben?
was	—

Inanimate nouns tend not to be used as indirect objects. Therefore, **was**, which refers to inanimate objects, is not used as an indirect object, and so an example sentence cannot be formed with that pronoun.

Übung   4-1

Rewrite each sentence, changing the word or phrase in boldface to the appropriate dative pronoun.

1. Er konnte **dem Polizisten** nicht antworten.

   _____

2. Ein Heft und Bleistifte nützen **einem neuen Schüler**.

   _____

3. Wir haben es **dem alten Herrn** gegeben.

   _____

4. Ein kleines Segelboot hat sich **der Insel** genähert.

   _____

5. Ich werde **meiner Schwester** ein paar Blumen kaufen.

   _____

6. Das wird **den Diplomaten** nicht imponieren.

   _____

7. Martin schenkte es **meinen Freunden und mir**.

   _____

8. Der Hund ist **der armen Frau** wieder entlaufen.

   _____

9. Kannst du **diesen Touristen** helfen?

   _____

10. Der Professor schreibt **jedem Studenten** einen kurzen Brief.

    _____

Übung   4-2

Rewrite each sentence in the present tense, substituting the pronouns **ich**, **du**, **wir**, **ihr**, *and* **Sie** *for the noun or third-person pronoun in boldface.*

1. Wer kann es **den Lehrlingen** erklären?

   a. (ich) _____

b. (du)   _____

c. (wir)   _____

d. (ihr)   _____

e. (Sie)   _____

2. Der Manager hat **ihm** ein Telegramm geschickt.

a. (ich)   _____

b. (du)   _____

c. (wir)   _____

d. (ihr)   _____

e. (Sie)   _____

3. Was haben sie **ihr** geschenkt?

a. (ich)   _____

b. (du)   _____

c. (wir)   _____

d. (ihr)   _____

e. (Sie)   _____

The dative case is also used as the object of dative verbs. German has a large number of dative verbs; those most commonly used are given below.

Infinitive

antworten	*to answer*
begegnen	*to encounter*
danken	*to thank*
dienen	*to serve*
entlaufen	*to run away (from)*
folgen	*to follow*
gehorchen	*to obey*
gehören	*to belong (to)*
glauben	*to believe*
gratulieren	*to congratulate*
helfen	*to help*
imponieren	*to impress*
raten	*to advise*
sagen	*to say, tell*

The noun or pronoun object of a dative verb must be in the dative case.

> Seine Dissertation hat **dem Professor** sehr imponiert.
> *His dissertation really impressed the professor.*

> Diese Handschuhe gehören **mir**.
> *These gloves belong to me.*

> Ich kann **euch** nicht helfen.
> *I can't help you.*

Because the concept of dative verbs does not exist in English, it is important that English speakers be aware of dative verbs in German. The dative object of a German sentence with a dative verb is often translated as a direct object in English. Since German direct objects are typically in the accusative case, English speakers sometimes mistakenly use that case where the dative case is needed in German.

> Wir helfen **ihnen**. (**ihnen** = dative object)
> *We help **them**. (**them** = direct object)*

> Glaubst du **ihm**? (**ihm** = dative object)
> *Do you believe **him**? (**him** = direct object)*

When a pronoun replaces a noun that is in the dative case, the pronoun must have the same gender and number as the noun.

> Seine Kusine hat **Hans** einen Brief geschrieben.
> *His cousin wrote Hans a letter.*
> Seine Kusine hat **ihm** einen Brief geschrieben.
> *His cousin wrote him a letter.*

> Wir geben **der Frau** ein Brot.
> *We give the woman a loaf of bread.*
> Wir geben **ihr** ein Brot.
> *We give her a loaf of bread.*

> Er erzählte es **dem Kind**.
> *He told it to the child.*
> Er erzählte es **ihm**.
> *He told it to him.*

> Ich gehorche **meinen Eltern**.
> *I obey my parents.*
> Ich gehorche **ihnen**.
> *I obey them.*

Übung	4-3

Rewrite each sentence, changing the dative pronoun to any appropriate noun or phrase.

1. Herr Schneider hat es mir gesagt.

_____

2. Das hat ihnen sehr imponiert.

_____

3. Was schenkst du ihr?

_____

4. Die Verkäuferin hat uns die neueste Mode gezeigt.

_____

5. Angelika macht euch eine kleine Überraschung.

_____

6. Hat er dir geantwortet?

_____

7. Zuerst müssen wir ihm die Jacke ausziehen.

_____

8. Morgen geben wir es Ihnen.

_____

Übung   4-4

Rewrite each sentence as a question, replacing the word or phrase in boldface with **wem**.

1. Ich habe **einem alten Freund** geholfen.

_____

2. Dieses Fahrrad gehört **der neuen Krankenschwester**.

_____

3. Der Reiseleiter hat es **uns** gezeigt.

_____

4. Wir können **euch** nicht glauben.

_____

5. Er folgt **mir**.

_____

6. Ich kann es **ihnen** nicht geben.

_____

7. Tante Angelika hat **ihm** eine neue Armbanduhr geschenkt.

_____

8. Der Hund ist **ihr** entlaufen.

_____

9. Martin kann **dir** helfen.

_____

10. Er wird es **uns** schicken.

_____

Übung   **4-5**

Circle the pronoun that best completes each sentence. Be careful! Some of the verbs require a dative pronoun, while others require an accusative pronoun.

1. Können Sie es _____ zeigen?   ihn | wir | mir

2. Ich brauche _____ für meine Eltern.   es | dir | uns

3. Die Lehrlinge haben _____ helfen müssen.   Sie | sie | ihnen

4. Warum glauben sie _____ nicht?   ihn | dich | uns

5. Mein Vater erzählte _____ ein paar Märchen.   ihr | ihn | Sie

6. Dieses Hemd gehört _____.   sie | mir | ihn

7. Sie hat _____ nicht verstanden.   ihm | Ihnen | es

8. Es hat _____ nicht imponiert.   ihr | sie | dich

9. Sie konnte _____ nicht antworten.   sie | uns | es

10. Was hast du _____ gegeben?   ihn | ihnen | ich

Pronouns in Prepositional Phrases

English and German pronouns are generally used in the same way in prepositional phrases. In English, the pronoun becomes the object of the preposition and changes to its object form.

with me
about you
from her
to them

In German, the case of the prepositional object depends on the preposition itself. There are accusative prepositions, dative prepositions, accusative-dative prepositions, and genitive prepositions. For the most part, pronouns are not used in the genitive case and instead have a possessive form (see Unit 7).

Accusative Prepositions

bis	*until, up to*	gegen	*against*
durch	*through*	ohne	*without*
entlang	*along, down*	um	*around, about*
für	*for*	wider	*against, contrary to*

Accusative case pronouns are used with these prepositions.

für **mich**
gegen **ihn**
ohne **uns**
um **Sie**

> Es ist ein Geschenk **für dich**.   *It's a gift for you.*
> Kommst du **ohne ihn**?   *Are you coming without him?*

Questions that use an accusative preposition and ask *whom* require the use of the interrogative pronoun **wen**.

> Das Geschenk ist für deinen Vater.
> **Für wen** ist das Geschenk?
> *Whom is the gift for?*

Er hat gegen einen Freund gesprochen.
Gegen wen hat er gesprochen?
Whom did he speak against?

Unlike the other accusative prepositions, **entlang** follows its noun or pronoun object.

Der Weg führte den Fluss **entlang**.
The path went along the river.
Der Weg führte ihn **entlang**.
The path went along it.

Dative Prepositions

aus	*out, from*	nach	*after*
außer	*except (for)*	seit	*since*
bei	*at, by*	von	*from, of*
mit	*with*	zu	*to, for*
gegenüber	*opposite*		

Dative case pronouns are used with these prepositions.

mit **mir**
nach **ihr**
zu **euch**
von **ihnen**

Wir bekommen einen Brief **von ihm**.
We receive a letter from him.

Martin wohnt **bei ihnen**.
Martin lives at their house.

Questions that use a dative preposition and ask *whom* require the use of the interrogative pronoun **wem**.

Sie will mit Herrn Keller reden.
Mit wem will sie reden?
Whom does she want to talk with?

Wir gehen zu unseren Eltern.
Zu wem gehen wir?
Whose house are we going to?

Unlike the other dative prepositions, **gegenüber** usually follows its noun or pronoun object.

Dem Sofa **gegenüber** stand ein Tisch.
A table stood opposite the sofa.

Uns **gegenüber** stand ein Tisch.
A table stood opposite us.

Accusative-Dative Prepositions

Some prepositions can use two cases, the accusative and dative. The accusative case with these prepositions usually indicates *movement* and is generally used with verbs of motion. The dative case is used when the prepositions show *location*.

an	*at*	über	*over*
auf	*on, onto*	unter	*under*
hinter	*behind*	vor	*in front of, before*
in	*in, into*	zwischen	*between*
neben	*next to*		

> Ich laufe **in den** Garten. (*movement [accusative case noun]*)
> *I run into the garden.*
> Ich sitze **im** (**in dem**) Garten. (*location [dative case noun]*)
> *I sit in the garden.*
>
> Erik stellt sich hinter **ihn**. (*movement [accusative case pronoun]*)
> *Erik places himself behind him.*
> Erik steht hinter **ihm**. (*location [dative case pronoun]*)
> *Erik stands behind him.*

The dative case is sometimes avoided and the accusative case is used instead, even where movement is not involved. This is because the dative case in such situations would imply a location— a meaning that would be absurd.

> Wir warten **auf ihn**.
> *We wait for him.* (We are not located **on** him.)
>
> Ich erinnere mich **an sie**.
> *I remember her.* (I am not located **at** her.)

Wen and **wem** are used with the accusative-dative prepositions when asking a question.

> **Auf wen** warten Sie?
> *Whom are you waiting for?*
>
> **Hinter wem** stand der Dieb?
> *Whom was the thief standing behind?*

In all prepositional phrases with **wen** or **wem**, the preposition must precede the pronoun and cannot be the last element in the sentence (unlike in English).

See Appendix B for a list of prepositions and the cases they require.

Übung   **5-1**

Rewrite each sentence, changing the word or phrase in boldface to the appropriate pronoun.

1. Ich habe für **Herrn Schneider** gearbeitet.

_____

2. Obwohl er schon 30 Jahre alt ist, wohnt er noch bei **seinen Eltern**.

_____

3. Wie lange müssen wir auf **den Professor** warten?

_____

4. Der Knabe hat sich immer vor **seinem alten Onkel** gefürchtet.

_____

5. Die alte Frau sehnte sich nach **ihrer jüngsten Tochter**.

_____

6. Ich habe ein paar Briefe von **Angelika** bekommen.

_____

7. Die tapferen Soldaten kämpfen gegen **die Feinde**.

_____

8. Es bestand ein großer Altersunterschied zwischen **den Schwestern**.

_____

9. Die Touristen lachen über **den komischen Mann**.

_____

10. Es ist fremdartig, dass Herr Keller ohne **seine Frau** kommt.

_____

Übung	5-2

Rewrite each incomplete sentence, inserting the appropriate form of the pronoun in parentheses.

1. Die Polizisten haben nach _____ gerufen.

   a. (ich)   _____

   b. (er)   _____

   c. (Sie)   _____

   d. (wir)   _____

   e. (ihr)   _____

2. Warum spotten die Mädchen über _____?

   a. (du)   _____

   b. (sie [*sing.*]) _____

c. (sie [*pl.*]) _____

d. (er) _____

e. (ich) _____

3. Oma sorgt sich immer um _____ .

a. (wir) _____

b. (ich) _____

c. (du) _____

d. (sie [*sing.*]) _____

e. (ihr) _____

Übung | **5-3**

Rewrite each sentence as a question, beginning each one with the preposition in boldface and the appropriate interrogative pronoun.

EXAMPLE   Er spricht **mit** ihr.

_____*Mit wem spricht er?*_____

1. Karin hat ein Geschenk **für** dich.

_____

2. Sie hat diese Gedichte **von** ihm bekommen.

_____

3. Die Kinder scheuten sich **vor** uns.

_____

4. Der Pförtner passt **auf** sie auf.

_____

5. Frau Gärtner hat oft **an** ihre ehemaligen Schüler gedacht.

_____

6. Wir haben die Nachricht **über** einen alten Freund geschickt.

_____

7. Das junge Ehepaar wohnte **bei** einer alten Witwe.

_____

8. Ludwig hat **nach** einem alten Klassenkameraden gefragt.

_____

9. Der junge Mann fährt **zu** seiner Verlobten.

_____

10. Das schüchterne Mädchen stellt sich **neben** ihren Vater.

_____

Unit 6

Direct and Indirect Object Pronouns in the Same Sentence

Both English and German exhibit quirkiness in word order when a sentence contains both a direct and an indirect object pronoun. In English, as long as the direct object is a noun, the indirect object—whether noun or pronoun—precedes the direct object.

Indirect object	Direct object	
I want to give **the letter carrier**	**these letters**.	(direct object = noun)
I want to give **him**	**these letters**.	(direct object = noun)

However, if the direct object is a pronoun, the indirect object—whether noun or pronoun—follows the direct object pronoun and is the object of the preposition *to* or *for*.

Direct object	Object of preposition	
I want to give **them**	**to the letter carrier**.	(direct object = pronoun)
I want to give **them**	**to him**.	(direct object = pronoun)

In German, direct and indirect object pronouns behave similarly. If the direct object is a noun, the indirect object—whether noun or pronoun—precedes the direct object. If the direct object is a pronoun, the indirect object—whether noun or pronoun—follows the direct object pronoun. And the indirect object always remains in the dative case and does not become the object of a preposition.

	Indirect object	Direct object		
Ich will	**dem Briefträger**	**diese Briefe**	geben.	(direct object = noun)
Ich will	**ihm**	**diese Briefe**	geben.	(direct object = noun)

	Direct object	Indirect object		
Ich will	**sie**	**dem Briefträger**	geben.	(direct object = pronoun)
Ich will	**sie**	**ihm**	geben.	(direct object = pronoun)

Übung	6-1

Rewrite each sentence, changing the indirect object in boldface to the appropriate pronoun.

1. Sie haben **dem jungen Lehrer** die neue Landkarte gezeigt.

   _____

2. Wirst du **Frau Schmidt** eine Flasche Milch geben?

   _____

3. Er bringt **seiner Verlobten** ein paar rote Nelken.

   _____

4. Ich habe es **meinen Verwandten in Leipzig** geschickt.

   _____

5. Marianne gab **Helga und mir** die alte Mundharmonika.

   _____

6. Er schenkte **den polnischen Touristen** Ansichtskarten.

   _____

7. Sie verkauft **dem armen Mann** den alten VW.

   _____

8. Leiht er **seiner Schwester** das Fahrrad?

   _____

9. Wir teilten **den Reisenden** die neuesten Nachrichten mit.

   _____

10. Die Räuber raubten **dem Wanderer** die Geldtasche.

    _____

Of course, if you are dealing with indirect object pronouns other than third-person pronouns, there are no nouns to consider, because only third-person pronouns (**er**, **sie** [*sing.*], **es**, and **sie** [*pl.*]) replace nouns. The pronouns **ich**, **du**, **wir**, **ihr**, and **Sie** are not replacements for nouns. And since direct object nouns in sentences that have indirect objects tend to be inanimate nouns, only third-person pronouns can be used as replacements.

Die Reiseleiterin zeigte ihm **das Gemälde**.
The tour guide showed him the painting.
Die Reiseleiterin zeigte **es** ihm. (*to him*)

Die Reiseleiterin zeigte ihr **das Gebäude**.
The tour guide showed her the building.
Die Reiseleiterin zeigte **es** ihr.

Die Reiseleiterin zeigte mir **die Bibliothek**.
The tour guide showed me the library.
Die Reiseleiterin zeigte **sie** mir.

Die Reiseleiterin zeigte dir **den Hafen**.
The tour guide showed you the harbor.
Die Reiseleiterin zeigte **ihn** dir.

Die Reiseleiterin zeigte uns **das Museum**.
The tour guide showed us the museum.
Die Reiseleiterin zeigte **es** uns.

Die Reiseleiterin zeigte euch **den Weg**.
The tour guide showed you the path.
Die Reiseleiterin zeigte **ihn** euch.

Die Reiseleiterin zeigte ihnen **die Bilder**.
The tour guide showed them the pictures.
Die Reiseleiterin zeigte **sie** ihnen.

Die Reiseleiterin zeigte Ihnen **das Theater**.
The tour guide showed you the theater.
Die Reiseleiterin zeigte **es** Ihnen.

Übung 6-2

Rewrite each sentence, changing the direct object in boldface to the appropriate pronoun.

1. Frau Schneider reicht dem Gast **einen Teller**.

_____

2. Meine Eltern haben dem Kellner **die Rechnung** bezahlt.

_____

3. Der junge Mann wird der alten Dame **seinen Platz** überlassen.

_____

4. Können Sie den Touristen **den Weg dorthin** zeigen?

   _____

5. Sie gibt dem Zahnarzt **das Geld**.

   _____

6. Wirst du deiner Frau **diesen Ring** schenken?

   _____

7. Ich kann den Pferden **das Futter** geben.

   _____

8. Mutti wird dem Kind **das schmutzige Hemd** ausziehen.

   _____

9. Wer schickte Hans **dieses Paket**?

   _____

10. Der Taschendieb verweigerte dem Rechtsanwalt **seine Antwort**.

   _____

Übung   6-3

Rewrite each sentence, changing both the direct and indirect objects in boldface to the appropriate pronouns.

1. Ich reiche **dem Besucher ein Glas Wasser**.

   _____

2. Doktor Schuhmann hat **dem alten Herrn das Rauchen** verboten.

   _____

3. Unsere Eltern haben **Martin und mir neue Stiefel** geschenkt.

   _____

4. Die Kellnerin bringt **den Gästen Brot, Butter und Käse**.

   _____

5. Haben Sie **der Frau eine Eintrittskarte** gegeben?

   _____

When the indirect object is the interrogative pronoun **wem**, there is no change in the word order of the direct object, whether it is a noun or pronoun. The only change required is the reversal of position of the subject and the verb. The verb precedes the subject in questions.

> **Wem** gibst du diese Blumen?
> *Whom are you giving these flowers to?*
> **Wem** gibst du sie?
> *Whom are you giving them to?*

When a question begins with **was** and that question contains an indirect object, there is no change in word order, whether the indirect object is a noun or pronoun.

> **Was** hast du dem Mann gezeigt?
> *What did you show the man?*
> **Was** hast du ihm gezeigt?
> *What did you show him?*

Remember that a noun plus the pronoun **ich** used as one phrase (for example, **meine Mutter und ich** and **die Kinder und ich**) change to a form of **wir** when used as a pronoun.

von meinem Vater und mir → von **uns**
einen Freund und mich   → **uns**

Übung   6-4

In the blank, write the appropriate form of the pronoun in parentheses. Be sure to use the appropriate case.

1. (ich)   Mein Vetter wird _____ eine Armbanduhr geben.

2. (du)   Der Dieb hat _____ auch einen teuren Ring geraubt.

3. (sie [*sing.*]) Ich kaufte _____ meinem Mann.

4. (wir)   Können Sie _____ das Schlafzimmer zeigen?

5. (ihr)   Eure Eltern werden _____ diese Ungezogenheit vergeben.

6. (sie [*pl.*])   Tante Gerda hat _____ ein paar alte Märchen erzählt.

7. (er)   Die Verkäuferin zeigte _____ die neuen Waren.

8. (Sie)   Der Chef wird _____ so eine Reise nie erlauben.

9. (sie [*sing.*]) Ich teile _____ die neuesten Nachrichten mit.

10. (er)   Ingrid schreibt _____ ihren Eltern.

Übung   **6-5**

Circle the pronoun that best completes each sentence.

1. Was habt ihr _____ gegeben?   mich | ihm | Sie

2. Martin wollte _____ dem Briefträger geben.   sie | ihnen | dir

3. _____ haben Sie ihm gezeigt?   Ihn | Wem | Was

4. Wir werden _____ die Nachrichten mitteilen.   euch | Sie | dich

5. Der alte Hund war _____ treu.   dich | wir | ihr

6. Der Reisende hat _____ verloren.   sie | ihm | ihnen

7. Der Lehrer hat _____ gelobt.   mir | uns | Sie

8. Der Junge hat _____ schon gelernt.   es | dir | ihr

9. Sie zeigte _____ dem jungen Arzt.   ihm | ihr | ihn

10. Kannst du _____ einen Schlips leihen?   dich | sie | mir

Possessive Pronouns

You may have noticed that the genitive case of pronouns has not been introduced thus far. In German, personal pronouns form a possessive pronoun as their genitive case form. And, just like English pronouns, German possessive pronouns are derived from the personal pronouns but are used like modifiers. The following chart summarizes this formation in English.

Subject pronoun	Object pronoun	Possessive
I	*me*	*my, mine*
you	*you*	*your, yours*
he	*him*	*his, his*
she	*her*	*her, hers*
it	*it*	*its, its*
we	*us*	*our, ours*
they	*them*	*their, theirs*
who	*whom*	*whose, whose*

Notice that English has two possessive forms. The first form listed modifies a noun that follows it; the other replaces the possessive and the noun that follows it and stands alone.

Possessive followed by noun	Possessive replacement
Whose book is that?	*Whose is that?*
My car was stolen!	*Mine was stolen!*
Where are their gloves?	*Where are theirs?*

German possessive pronouns are quite similar to their English counterparts. Although there are three distinct cases of personal pronouns to consider (nominative, accusative, and dative), the possessive derived from the personal pronouns has its own unique form and is used as a modifier. As such, it can be used in all four cases (nominative, accusative, dative, and genitive). Just like English, German has two possessive forms.

Nominative	Accusative	Dative	Possessive
ich	mich	mir	mein, meiner
du	dich	dir	dein, deiner
er	ihn	ihm	sein, seiner
sie	sie	ihr	ihr, ihrer
es	es	ihm	sein, seiner
wir	uns	uns	unser, unsrer
ihr	euch	euch	euer, eurer
sie	sie	ihnen	ihr, ihrer
Sie	Sie	Ihnen	Ihr, Ihrer

Since German possessives are modifiers, they must have the appropriate ending for the gender, number, and case of the noun they modify.

Nominative

Masculine	**mein** guter Freund	*my good friend*
Feminine	**meine** alte Großmutter	*my old grandmother*
Neuter	**mein** neues Auto	*my new car*
Plural	**meine** teuren Ringe	*my expensive rings*

Accusative

Masculine	**ihren** netten Lehrer	*her nice teacher*
Feminine	**ihre** rote Bluse	*her red blouse*
Neuter	**ihr** neues Haus	*her new house*
Plural	**ihre** deutschen Verwandten	*her German relatives*

Dative

Masculine	**seinem** blauen Rennwagen	*his blue racing car*
Feminine	**seiner** kleinen Landkarte	*his little map*
Neuter	**seinem** ersten Gedicht	*his first poem*
Plural	**seinen** guten Freunden	*his good friends*

Genitive

Masculine	**deines** kleinen Bruders	*of your little brother*
Feminine	**deiner** schönen Schwester	*of your pretty sister*
Neuter	**deines** neuen Flugzeugs	*of your new airplane*
Plural	**deiner** blauen Augen	*of your blue eyes*

Third-person singular and plural nouns in the genitive case can be replaced by the corresponding possessive modifier.

Masculine	**sein**
Feminine	**ihr**
Neuter	**sein**
Plural	**ihr**

Der Hut **des alten Mannes** ist schwarz.
The old man's hat is black.
Sein Hut ist schwarz.
His hat is black.

Die Katze **dieser Frau** war krank.
This woman's cat was sick.
Ihre Katze war krank.
Her cat was sick.

Der Ton **des Gedichts** ist traurig.
The tone of the poem is sad.
Sein Ton ist traurig.
Its tone is sad.

Die Pässe **der Touristen** sind nicht gültig.
The tourists' passports aren't valid.
Ihre Pässe sind nicht gültig.
Their passports aren't valid.

Übung	7-1

Rewrite each sentence, changing the word or phrase in boldface to the appropriate possessive modifier.

EXAMPLE   Wo ist die Tasche **der alten Frau**?

     Wo ist ihre Tasche?

1. Kennst du den Bruder **des neuen Studenten**?

   _____

2. Die Rede **des Bundeskanzlers** war ziemlich interessant.

   _____

3. Die Stimme **des schüchternen Kindes** war so weich.

   _____

4. Das Schlafzimmer **der jüngsten Tochter** ist zu klein.

   _____

5. Ist die Aktentasche **des Rechtsanwalts** noch im Büro?

   _____

6. Die Klassenzimmer **dieser Lehrerinnen** sind im zweiten Stock.

   _____

7. Haben Sie das Gebrüll **des alten Löwen** gehört?

   _____

8. Das Spielzeug **der Mädchen** lag überall auf dem Fußboden.

_____

9. Ich erkannte sofort das Gesicht **des Verbrechers**.

_____

10. Wo ist der Schreibtisch **der neuen Stenographistin**?

_____

Übung   7-2

Rewrite each sentence, replacing the possessive pronoun in boldface with the possessive modifier equivalent of the subject pronoun of the sentence.

EXAMPLE   Er besucht **deinen** Bruder.

_____Er besucht seinen Bruder._____

1. Sie hat **meine** neue Telefonnummer vergessen.

_____

2. Wo hast du **ihren** Hund gefunden?

_____

3. Ich steckte das Geld in **seine** Tasche.

_____

4. Wir hängen **dein** Bild an die Wand.

_____

5. Werdet ihr **meine** Verwandten in Bayern besuchen?

_____

6. Wohnen Sie noch bei **seinen** Freunden?

_____

7. Haben sie **unserer** Bekannten in Berlin geschrieben?

_____

8. Sie sah **seinen** Hut aus dem Fenster des Autos verschwinden.

_____

9. Wir haben das Rathaus **eurer** Stadt verbrennen sehen.

_____

10. Ich habe **deine** Schwester nicht geschlagen.

_____

If the noun is omitted and the possessive stands alone as its replacement, it must still retain the gender, number, and case of the noun. In this form, it is no longer a modifier, but a pronoun.

Deine Eltern sind zu Hause, aber **unsere** sind jetzt verreist. (unsere Eltern)
Your parents are at home, but ours are traveling now.

Du kennst meinen Bruder, aber ich kenne **deinen** nicht. (deinen Bruder)
You know my brother, but I don't know yours.

Sein Gedicht ist ziemlich gut, aber **ihres** ist viel besser. (ihr Gedicht)
His poem is rather good, but hers is much better.

„Ist das Ihr Wagen?" „Ja, das ist **meiner**." (mein Wagen)
"Is that your car?" "Yes, that's mine."

Two additional forms of the possessive can replace a possessive that modifies a noun and act as a new noun, although they are less common and are found in more traditional and literary language. They are shown below in boldface.

Personal	Possessive	Noun 1	Noun 2
ich	mein	**der meine**	**der meinige**
du	dein	**der deine**	**der deinige**
er	sein	**der seine**	**der seinige**
sie	ihr	**der ihre**	**der ihrige**
es	sein	**der seine**	**der seinige**
wir	unser	**der unsere**	**der unsrige**
ihr	euer	**der eure**	**der eurige**
sie	ihr	**der ihre**	**der ihrige**
Sie	Ihr	**der Ihre**	**der Ihrige**

The possessive forms in the last two columns above must retain the gender, number, and case of the noun they replace. These words are identified as nouns because they require a definite article. Keep in mind that the high-frequency form is the possessive introduced earlier (**mein/ meiner, dein/deiner**, etc.).

The interrogative pronoun **wer** merits special consideration. It has an accusative case form (**wen**) and a dative case form (**wem**), and like the other pronouns, its genitive case form is a possessive pronoun, **wessen**. But unlike the other possessive pronouns, which must conform to the gender, number, and case of the noun they replace, the genitive case form of the interrogative pronoun has only the one form: **wessen**.

Nominative masculine
_____

Wessen Wagen ist das?
Whose car is that?

Accusative feminine

Wessen Tasche haben Sie gefunden?
Whose purse did you find?

Dative plural

Mit **wessen** Kindern hat er gesprochen?
With whose children did he speak?

Übung	7-3

Rewrite each sentence as a question, replacing the possessive modifier or pronoun in boldface with **wessen.**

EXAMPLE   **Sein** Hut ist zu klein.

Wessen Hut ist zu klein?

1. **Ihr** Fahrrad ist gestern Nacht gestohlen worden.

_____

2. **Meine** Enkelkinder werden bald zu Besuch kommen.

_____

3. Niemand kann **seine** Frage beantworten.

_____

4. Karl hat mit **unserer** Kusine getanzt.

_____

5. Wir werden nur noch ein paar Minuten auf **deine** Schwestern warten.

_____

6. **Ihr** Wecker ist zu laut.

_____

7. Sie haben versucht **seinem** Großvater zu helfen.

_____

8. Der Student will bei **euren** Eltern wohnen.

_____

9. **Ihres** ist zu klein.

_____

10. Frau Schäfer möchte **meinen** Professor kennen lernen.

_____

Rewrite each sentence, changing the possessive pronoun standing alone to a possessive modifier followed by an appropriate noun or phrase.

EXAMPLE   Ihres ist zu klein.

Ihr neues Haus ist zu klein.   _____

1. Wo ist denn meiner?

_____

2. Wir haben deinen nicht erkannt.

_____

3. Herr Bauer hat seines nicht gefunden.

_____

4. Die Kinder spielen mit ihren.

_____

5. Kann niemand unserem helfen?

_____

6. Ist Ihre krank?

_____

7. Ich beschäftige mich mit meiner.

_____

8. Angelika denkt an deinen.

_____

9. Warum liest du nicht in deinem?

_____

10. Sie sieht ihren.

_____

Einer/Keiner and Interrogatives Used as Pronouns

Einer and Keiner

In Unit 7, you learned that possessive pronouns can function as modifiers and that they can also replace a noun and function as a true pronoun. These functions also occur with **ein** and **kein**. English uses *one* and *none* similarly.

Modifier	Pronoun
One child is quite sick.	*One* is quite sick.
One problem is the lack of water.	*One* is the lack of water.
I don't have *a quarter*.	I don't have *one*.
No person has a right to say that.	*No one* has a right to say that.
I met *no interesting people* there.	I met *none* there.
There's *no money* left.	There's *none* left.

To change *one* or *a* + a noun (animate or inanimate) to a pronoun, you use *one*. When changing *no* + an animate noun to a pronoun, you can use *no one, nobody,* or *none*. When changing *no* + an inanimate noun to a pronoun, you can use *nothing* or *none*.

German is less complicated: **Einer** replaces **ein** + any noun, and **keiner** replaces **kein** + any noun. German requires that the pronouns **einer** and **keiner** retain the gender, number, and case of the noun they replace. The following pairs of sentences illustrate **einer** and **keiner** used as a modifier and as a pronoun.

Modifier	Pronoun
Ein neuer Lehrer wohnt hier.	**Einer** wohnt hier.
A new teacher lives here.	*A new one lives here.*

Modifier	Pronoun
Siehst du **eine alte Kirche**?	Siehst du **eine**?
Do you see an old church?	*Do you see one?*
Ich habe **ein Ei** gefunden.	Ich habe **eines** gefunden.
I found one egg.	*I found one.*
Sie spricht mit **einem Soldaten**.	Sie spricht mit **einem**.
She speaks with a soldier.	*She speaks with one.*
Keine Ausländer sind da.	**Keine** sind da.
No foreigners are there.	*None are there.*
Sie verhaften **keinen Dieb**.	Sie verhaften **keinen**.
They arrest no thief.	*They arrest none.*
Kein Mensch hilft uns.	**Keiner** hilft uns.
Not a person helps us.	*No one helps us.*
Er glaubt **keinen Politikern**.	Er glaubt **keinen**.
He believes no politicians.	*He believes none.*

When **einer** and **keiner** are used as pronouns, their declension is slightly different from when they modify a noun directly. This difference occurs in the masculine and neuter forms of the nominative and accusative.

	Masculine with noun		Masculine as pronoun	
Nominative	ein Mann	kein Mann	ein**er**	kein**er**
Accusative	einen Mann	keinen Mann	einen	keinen
Dative	einem Mann	keinem Mann	einem	keinem
Genitive	eines Mannes	keines Mannes	—	—

	Feminine with noun		Feminine as pronoun	
Nominative	eine Frau	keine Frau	eine	keine
Accusative	eine Frau	keine Frau	eine	keine
Dative	einer Frau	keiner Frau	einer	keiner
Genitive	einer Frau	keiner Frau	—	—

	Neuter with noun		Neuter as pronoun	
Nominative	ein Kind	kein Kind	ein**es**	kein**es**
Accusative	ein Kind	kein Kind	ein**es**	kein**es**
Dative	einem Kind	keinem Kind	einem	keinem
Genitive	eines Kindes	keines Kindes	—	—

	Plural with noun		Plural as pronoun	
Nominative	—	keine Kinder	—	keine
Accusative	—	keine Kinder	—	keine
Dative	—	keinen Kindern	—	keinen
Genitive	—	keiner Kinder	—	—

Notice that the genitive case is not used when these words are used as pronouns. Also, be aware that **einer** is only used as a replacement for *singular nouns*.

Übung   8-1

Rewrite each sentence, changing the noun phrase in boldface to the appropriate form of **einer** *and* **keiner**.

EXAMPLE   Der Mann ist sehr stark.

a. *Einer ist sehr stark.*

b. *Keiner ist sehr stark.*

1. Wir werden **unseren neuen Nachbarn** besuchen.

   a. _____

   b. _____

2. **Einige Touristen** sind in der Kunsthalle geblieben.

   a. _____

   b. _____

3. Ich habe **eine sehr gute Idee**.

   a. _____

   b. _____

4. Hast du **ein Brot** gekauft?

   a. _____

   b. _____

5. **Viele Leute** wollen nach Ägypten reisen.

   a. _____

   b. _____

6. Erhardt hat **einen gebrauchten Fotoapparat** gekauft.

   a. _____

   b. _____

7. Marianne spielt mit **einer Katze**.

   a. _____

   b. _____

8. Im Sommer trägt eine Dame **ein leichtes Kleid**.

   a. _____

   b. _____

9. **Eine Frage** betrifft meinen älteren Bruder.

   a. _____

   b. _____

10. Die kleinen Schüler gehorchten **einem Lehrer**.

   a. _____

   b. _____

Interrogative Pronouns

Wer and *was*

You are already familiar with **wer** and **was**. They are pronouns that replace a noun and form a question that asks about the noun they replace.

> **Herr Bauer** hat sich den linken Arm gebrochen.
> *Mr. Bauer broke his left arm.*
> **Wer** hat sich den linken Arm gebrochen?
> *Who broke his left arm?*

> Sie sehen **riesige Berge**.
> *They see gigantic mountains.*
> **Was** sehen sie?
> *What do they see?*

For the interrogative **wer**, you must consider the case of the noun that this pronoun replaces; if it replaces a possessive pronoun or a genitive noun, you must use the appropriate possessive form of **wer** (**wessen**). **Was**, however, has only one form.

Nominative case

Das Kind weint.	**Wer** weint?
The child is crying.	*Who is crying?*
Ein Sturm kommt.	**Was** kommt?
A storm is coming.	*What is coming?*

Accusative case

Sie kennt **meinen Onkel**.	**Wen** kennt sie?
She knows my uncle.	*Whom does she know?*
Er kaufte **einen BMW**.	**Was** kaufte er?
He bought a BMW.	*What did he buy?*

Dative case

Sie haben **ihr** geholfen.	**Wem** haben Sie geholfen?
They helped her.	*Whom did they help?*
Er schreibt **mit einem Bleistift**.	**Womit** schreibt er?
He writes with a pencil.	*What does he write with?*

Genitive case/possessive

Hans hat **ihre** Tasche gefunden.	**Wessen** Tasche hat Hans gefunden?
Hans found her purse.	*Whose purse did Hans find?*
Die Farbe **des Autos** ist blau.	**Wessen** Farbe ist blau?
The color of the car is blue.	*Whose color (The color of what . . .) is blue?*

Remember that inanimate nouns in a prepositional phrase must become prepositional adverbs when they are replaced by pronouns.

> Er schreibt **mit einem Bleistift**.
> *He writes with a pencil.*
> Er schreibt **damit**.
> *He writes with it.*
> **Womit** schreibt er?
> *What does he write with?*

Prepositional adverbs such as **damit** and **womit** will be treated in detail in Unit 18.

Übung 8-2

Rewrite each sentence as a question, replacing the word or phrase in boldface with the appropriate form of **wer** *or* **was**.

EXAMPLE   Er findet **eine Briefmarke**.

_____*Was findet er?*_____

1. Die Jungen haben **ein paar Äpfel** gegessen.

   _____

2. Er fütterte **sein** Pferd.

   _____

3. Der alte Professor soll **jeden Studenten** prüfen.

   _____

4. Der Reporter hat mit **dem Bundeskanzler** gesprochen.

   _____

5. Die Mädchen sahen **ihre Freundinnen** dort spielen und schwimmen.

   _____

6. Das Kind konnte **die Weintrauben** nicht erreichen.

   _____

7. Klaudia hat **ihre** Eltern vorgestellt.

_____

8. Tante Luise hat ein Geschenk **für Martin** gekauft.

_____

Welcher

The word **welcher** asks *which* or *what* of a noun when it is a modifier.

> **Welches** Haus habt ihr gekauft?
> *Which house did you buy?*

> **Welche** Antwort ist die Richtige?
> *What answer is the correct one?*

But **welcher** can also be used as a pronoun, like **einer** or **keiner**. Like **einer** and **keiner**, it must retain the gender, number, and case of the noun it replaces.

> **Welche** Bücher hast du gefunden?
> *Which books did you find?*
> **Welche** hast du gefunden?
> *Which did you find?*

> **Welchen** Mann haben sie verhaftet?
> *Which man did they arrest?*
> **Welchen** haben sie verhaftet?
> *Which one did they arrest?*

> Von **welchem** Gast ist dieses Geschenk?
> *Which guest is this gift from?*
> Von **welchem** ist dieses Geschenk?
> *Which one is this gift from?*

Unlike **einer** and **keiner**, which have a slightly different declension in the masculine and neuter nominative and accusative when used as pronouns, **welcher** has the same endings whether it is used as a modifier or a pronoun. But like **einer** and **keiner**, **welcher** as a pronoun has no genitive form. The following chart shows the masculine declension of **welcher** when used as a modifier and as a pronoun.

	Modifier	Pronoun
Nominative	welcher Lehrer	welcher
Accusative	welchen Lehrer	welchen
Dative	welchem Lehrer	welchem
Genitive	welches Lehrers	—

As you can see, it is not just the personal pronouns that can replace nouns; a variety of other words also can. Words that replace nouns are pronouns.

Übung   8-3

Rewrite each sentence as a question, using the appropriate form of **welcher** *to replace the noun or prepositional phrase in boldface. First, write a question using* **welcher** *as a modifier, then write a question using it as a pronoun.*

EXAMPLE   Er kaufte **einen roten Wagen**.

a.   *Welchen Wagen kaufte er?*

b.   *Welchen kaufte er?*

1. Johann hat ihr **die schönsten Blumen** geschenkt.

    a. _____

    b. _____

2. Die Theaterbesucher wollten sich **mit der berühmten Schauspielerin** treffen.

    a. _____

    b. _____

3. **Ein großes Schiff** ist heute morgen von Bremerhaven abgefahren.

    a. _____

    b. _____

4. **Der alte Obstbaum** blüht jedes Jahr im April.

    a. _____

    b. _____

5. Die Bauern haben das Korn **in die neue Scheune** gebracht.

    a. _____

    b. _____

6. Die alten Pferde haben **den schweren Wagen** gezogen.

    a. _____

    b. _____

7. Die Lehrerin beobachtet **die kleinen Kinder** beim Spielen.

    a. _____

    b. _____

8. Der Fremdenführer hat **den amerikanischen Besuchern** das Museum gezeigt.

   a. _____

   b. _____

9. **Die Kugel des Räubers** verwundete einen alten Herrn.

   a. _____

   b. _____

10. Er hat **um ihren Mädchennamen** gebeten.

   a. _____

   b. _____

Determiners Used as Pronouns

Determiners as Modifiers and Pronouns

The words **ein**, **kein**, and **welch** are called determiners and function as modifiers. Several other determiners can be used as modifiers, and they can also be used as pronouns, just like **einer**, **keiner**, and **welcher**.

Derjenige, der and *derselbe*

Two such determiners, **derjenige, der** (*that very*) and **derselbe** (*the same*), are made up of two words to form a new meaning. They can modify a noun that follows them, or they can be used as pronouns; both can be of any gender, number, or case. **Derjenige, der** is generally followed by a relative clause.

Modifier	Er sprach mit **demjenigen** Mann, **der** ihm es raubte.
	He spoke with the very man who robbed him of it.
Pronoun	Er sprach mit **demjenigen, der** ihm es raubte.
	He spoke with the very one who robbed him of it.

Modifier	Hast du **dieselben** Schuhe gekauft?
	Did you buy the same shoes?
Pronoun	Hast du **dieselben** gekauft?
	Did you buy the same ones?

Notice that the English translation of many determiners requires adding *one(s)* to the basic meaning of the pronoun.

derjenige, der	*the very one who*
derselbe	*the same one*
keiner	*no one*
welcher	*which one*

Übung	9-1

Rewrite each sentence, changing the word in boldface to the appropriate form of **derjenige**.

EXAMPLE   Das ist **der** Mann, der mir folgte.

   Das ist derjenige Mann, der mir folgte.

1. Kennst du **jene** Frau, die für Herrn Bauer gearbeitet hat?

   _____

2. Er sprach mit **einem** Kind, das seine Mutter verloren hat.

   _____

3. **Dieses** Mädchen, von dem wir sprachen, ist eine Freundin von ihm.

   _____

4. Ich habe etwas für **den** Jungen, der weint.

   _____

5. Wir glauben **diesen** Leuten, die die fremdartige Geschichte erzählten.

   _____

Rewrite each of the following sentences, changing the word in boldface to the appropriate form of **derselbe**.

6. Gerhardt hat **keinen** Schlips gekauft.

   _____

7. Hast du dir **den** Finger wieder gebrochen?

   _____

8. Hans kommt von **einer** Stadt im Schwarzwald.

   _____

9. In **dem** Irrgarten sind sie wieder verloren gegangen.

   _____

10. Ich möchte **es**.

   _____

Dieser, jeder, and jener

The modifiers **dieser**, **jeder**, and **jener** can also be used as pronouns. The pronoun form of each of these words retains the gender, number, and case of the noun it replaces.

Modifier	**Dieses** Problem ist unglaublich schwer.
	This problem is incredibly difficult.
Pronoun	**Dieses** ist unglaublich schwer.
	This one is incredibly difficult.
Modifier	Der Professor hat **jeden** Studenten geprüft.
	The professor tested each student.
Pronoun	Der Professor hat **jeden** geprüft.
	The professor tested each one.
Modifier	Er verlebte das Wochenende mit **jenem** Freund.
	He spent the weekend with that friend.
Pronoun	Er verlebte das Wochenende mit **jenem**.
	He spent the weekend with that one.

Manch, solch, viel, welch, and wenig

Another group of determiners consists of **manch**, **solch**, **viel**, **welch**, and **wenig**. These five words can be used in a declined form (like **dieser**) and in an undeclined form when used before adjectives. However, when they are used as pronouns, they must be declined according to gender, number, and case.

Undeclined

Manch arme Frau führt ein schweres Leben.
Many a poor woman leads a hard life.

Gestern hatten wir **solch** gutes Wetter.
We had such good weather yesterday.

Sie kaufen **viel** buntes Material.
They're buying a lot of colorful material.

Welch frische Luft!
What fresh air!

Hier gibt es **wenig** interessante Bücher.
There are few interesting books here.

Declined

An **manchen** Tagen will ich einfach nicht aufstehen.
On some days, I simply don't want to get up.

Solchen Männern kann man leider nicht trauen.
Unfortunately, such men aren't to be trusted.

Viele Leute sind noch arbeitslos.
Many people are still unemployed.

Welche Handschuhe willst du?
Which gloves do you want?

Sie bleiben noch **wenige** Tage in Bremen.
They're staying a few days more in Bremen.

Pronoun

An **manchen** will ich einfach nicht aufstehen.
On some, I simply don't want to get up.

Solchen kann man leider nicht trauen.
Unfortunately, ones like that are not to be trusted.

Viele sind noch arbeitslos.
Many are still unemployed.

Welche willst du?
Which do you want?

Sie bleiben noch **wenige** in Bremen.
They'll stay a few more in Bremen.

The sentences in the last group are taken out of context. In conversation or writing, the omitted nouns would be understood and the sentences would make sense.

Note that **welch** in its undeclined form can be used in a statement. In its declined form, **welcher** is used in a question.

> **Welch** ein gutes Buch war das!
> *What a good book that was!*

> **Welches** Buch hast du gelesen?
> *Which book did you read?*

Alle, beide, einige, and mehrere

A few determiners are used primarily in the plural, but they, too, must retain the gender, number, and case of the noun they replace when they are used as pronouns. These words are **alle** (*all*), **beide** (*both*), **einige** (*some*), and **mehrere** (*several*).

Modifier

Alle Touristen besuchen die neue Kunsthalle.
All tourists visit the new art museum.

Wir werden **beide** Regenmäntel kaufen.
We're going to buy both raincoats.

Einige schwer verwundete Soldaten sind umgekommen.
Some of the badly wounded soldiers died.

Er hat sich mit **mehreren** Kandidaten unterhalten.
He conversed with several candidates.

Pronoun

Alle besuchen die neue Kunsthalle.
Everyone visits the new art museum.

Wir werden **beide** kaufen.
We're going to buy both.

Pronoun

Einige sind umgekommen.
Some died.

Er hat sich mit **mehreren** unterhalten.
He conversed with several.

Übung   9-2

Rewrite each sentence, changing the noun phrase in boldface to the appropriate pronoun form of the word in parentheses.

EXAMPLE   (dieser)   **Der Wagen** ist ein VW.

_____*Dieser ist ein VW.*_____

1. (dieser)   **Mein Lehrer** kommt aus England.

_____

2. (jeder)   Musst du dich in **einen reichen Mann** verlieben?

_____

3. (jener)   Ich habe **ein Haus** in der Marktstraße gekauft.

_____

4. (dieser)   Martin wollte **einen Artikel** übersetzen.

_____

5. (jeder)   Wir werden **unserem Vertreter in Berlin** schreiben.

_____

6. (jener)   Erich hat mit **der schönen Schauspielerin** getanzt.

_____

Übung   9-3

Rewrite each sentence, changing the noun phrase in boldface to the appropriate pronoun form of the word in parentheses.

EXAMPLE   (welcher)   Ist **der Wagen** ein VW?

_____*Welcher ist ein VW?*_____

1. (solcher)   Ich würde niemals **einen grünen Anzug** kaufen.

_____

2. (mancher)   **Alte Leute** werden häufiger krank.

_____

3. (viel)   Ich habe mit **euren Gästen** darüber gesprochen.

_____

4. (welcher)   **Ein gelbes** willst du haben?

_____

5. (wenig)   Das Theaterstück hat **den Kindern** gefallen.

_____

6. (alle)   **Keine Jungen** wollen mit dem Meister Schach spielen.

_____

7. (einige)   Ich kenne nur **drei oder vier Leute** hier.

_____

8. (mehrere)   Seine Zauberkraft hat **den Zuschauern** imponiert.

_____

9. (solcher)   Ich finde **diese Idee** albern.

_____

10. (alle)   Wir werden **unsere Verwandten** in der Schweiz besuchen.

_____

Alles, etwas, nichts, jemand, and niemand

Certain other commonly used pronouns are replacements for a variety of nouns, because they have a _general_ meaning and are not a _specific_ substitute for a noun. English has similar non-specific pronouns.

Sentence with a noun	Pronoun substitution
I'm holding the girl.	_I'm holding **her**._ (specific) _I'm holding **someone**._ (not specific)
I see a mountain.	_I see **it**._ (specific) _I see **something**._ (not specific)

This idea of a non-specific pronoun occurs in German with **alles** (*everything*), **etwas** (*something*), **nichts** (*nothing*), **jemand** (*someone*), and **niemand** (*no one*).

Noun	Non-specific pronoun
Das sind elf Bücher und eine Zeitschrift. *That's eleven books and one magazine.*	Das ist **alles**. *That's everything.*
Er trägt einen Koffer. *He's carrying a suitcase.*	Er trägt **etwas**. *He's carrying something.*
Ich habe kein Geld. *I have no money.*	Ich habe **nichts**. *I have nothing.*
Hast du einen Fremden da gesehen? *Did you see a stranger there?*	Hast du **jemand** da gesehen? *Did you see someone there?*
Keine Studenten konnten antworten. OR Die Studenten konnten nicht antworten. *The students couldn't answer.*	**Niemand** konnte antworten. *No one could answer.*

Both **jemand** and **niemand** can show an ending in the accusative and dative cases.

Nominative	Accusative	Dative
jemand	jemand OR jemanden	jemand OR jemandem
niemand	niemand OR niemanden	niemand OR niemandem

Notice also that in the sentence above that begins **Die Studenten ...**, niemand replaces a noun and a negative word.

> **Die Studenten** konnten **nicht** antworten.
> *The students couldn't answer.*
> **Niemand** konnte antworten.
> *No one could answer.*

When the pronoun **alles**, **etwas**, **nichts**, **jemand**, or **niemand** replaces a plural noun used as a subject, the verb is changed to the singular.

> Gabeln und Messer **liegen** auf dem Boden.
> *Forks and knives are on the floor.*
> Etwas **liegt** auf dem Boden.
> *Something is on the floor.*

Übung 9-4

Rewrite each sentence, changing the words in boldface to the appropriate pronoun that is a general *replacement for a noun. Choose from* **alles**, **etwas**, **nichts**, **jemand**, *and* **niemand**.

EXAMPLE   **Kein Mensch** wollte helfen.

　　　　　　　Niemand wollte helfen.

1. Ich habe **eine kleine Überraschung** für euch.

2. Der arme Junge hat **das ganze Gedicht** vergessen.

_____

3. Martin kennt **keinen einzigen Studenten** im Hörsaal.

_____

4. **Eine fremde Frau** stand an der Ecke und weinte.

_____

5. Warten Sie auf **die Touristen aus Kanada**?

_____

6. **Die Besucher** lachten **nicht** darüber.

_____

7. Er hat **seine Mappe, Bücher und Hefte** verloren.

_____

8. Wir werden **Vaters Chef** in Heidelberg treffen.

_____

9. Haben Sie **die Nachrichten** gehört?

_____

10. Der schüchterne Knabe will **keine Weihnachtslieder** singen.

_____

Übung 9-5

Rewrite each sentence, changing the pronoun in boldface to any appropriate noun or noun phrase. Retain the pronoun as a modifier wherever possible.

1. Wir werden **jeden** besuchen wollen.

_____

2. Sind **alle** wahnsinnig geworden?

_____

3. Ich treffe **diejenigen**, die mich verspottet hatten.

_____

4. **Beide** sind gute Freunde von mir.

_____

5. Hast du **etwas** für mich?

_____

6. Gudrun hat nur **wenige** kennen gelernt.

_____

7. **Einige** wohnen noch im Harzgebirge.

_____

8. Warum haben Sie **solches** ausgewählt?

_____

9. **Niemand** versteht mich.

_____

10. Meine Schwester möchte **dieselbe** haben.

_____

11. **Jemand** konnte die Frage beantworten.

_____

12. **Welche** haben Sie gekauft?

_____

13. **Diese** sind viel besser.

_____

14. Benno hat **dasselbe** gefunden.

_____

15. Werdet ihr **beide** verkaufen?

_____

Definite Articles as Pronouns

The definite article **der/die/das** is translated into English as *the*. But it can also function as a pronoun and tends to be used where the speaker wishes to be more emphatic.

„Hast du ihre letzte Vorlesung gehört?" „Ja, **die** war ausgezeichnet!"
"Did you hear her last lecture?" "Yes, it was excellent!"

In general, you can substitute a definite article for any third-person singular or plural pronoun. The declension of the definite article used as a pronoun, however, is slightly different from the declension of the definite article used before a noun.

Definite article

	Masculine	Feminine	Neuter	Plural
Nominative	der	die	das	die
Accusative	den	die	das	die
Dative	dem	der	dem	den
Genitive	des	der	des	der

Definite article as a pronoun

	Masculine	Feminine	Neuter	Plural
Nominative	der	die	das	die
Accusative	den	die	das	die
Dative	dem	der	dem	**denen**
Genitive	**dessen**	**deren**	**dessen**	**deren**

The genitive form is used to avoid confusion when a subject and object of the same gender are followed by a possessive of the same gender.

> Karin wollte mit ihrer Tante und **ihrer** Tochter sprechen.
> *Karin wanted to speak to her aunt and her (**Karin's**) daughter.*

> Karin wollte mit ihrer Tante und **deren** Tochter sprechen.
> *Karin wanted to speak with her aunt and her (**aunt's**) daughter.*

Übung 9-6

Rewrite each sentence, changing the noun or noun phrase in boldface to the appropriate form of the definite article used as a pronoun.

1. **Die Leute** haben keine Ahnung!

___

2. Ich möchte mit **dem Detektiv** sprechen.

___

3. Wir haben einen Brief von **Verwandten** in Polen bekommen.

___

4. Angelika kommt mit **einer neuen Bekannten**.

___

5. Die Katze schläft auf **einem Stuhl** in der Ecke.

___

The Pronoun *man*

The German indefinite pronoun **man** is generally translated into English as *one* or *you*. The English pronoun *one* has a more formal tone, and *you* sounds more casual.

> **One** *should be careful how* **one** *phrases* **one's** *sentences.*
> **You** *should be careful how* **you** *phrase* **your** *sentences.*

The German pronoun **man** is used in place of either of these English pronouns—but only in the nominative case. It stands for a person or people in general and is not a replacement for a specific noun.

> **Man** kann nicht jedem gefallen.
> *One cannot please everyone.*

> Wenn **man** nichts zu sagen hat, soll **man** lieber einfach
> schweigen?
> *If one has nothing to say, should one simply remain silent?*

But **man** goes beyond the translation of *one* and *you*. It is often used where English speakers use *someone* or *somebody*.

> **Man** steht an der Tür und klopft.
> *Someone is standing at the door knocking.*

> Kann **man** verstehen, was er versucht zu sagen?
> *Can somebody understand what he's trying to say?*

Since **man** cannot be used in any case but the nominative, what happens in the accusative and dative? The answer is simple: The pronoun is changed to **einer**.

> **Man** muss misstrauisch sein, wenn **einem** ein unerwartetes
> Geschenk gegeben wird.
> *One must be suspicious when one is given an unexpected gift.*

Man is also frequently used where English uses a clause in the passive voice. The equivalent German clause is stated in the active voice and uses **man** as its subject.

> **Man sagt**, dass es ihm gelingen wird.
> *It is said that he will succeed.*

Man wird sie dafür **verprügeln**.

*They **will be thrashed** for it.* (literally, *One will thrash them for it.*)

The pronoun **man** should not be confused with the noun **der Mann** (*the man*).

Übung	**10-1**

*Fill in each blank with **man** or an appropriate form of **einer**.*

1. Wenn _____ sich nicht wohl fühlt, soll _____ zu Hause bleiben.

2. Was _____ kauft, das soll _____ gefallen.

3. Hat _____ an der Ecke gewartet?

4. _____ behauptet, dass er ein Taschendieb war.

5. Wie kann _____ etwas anderes erwarten?

6. _____ soll dankbar sein, wenn _____ auch ein kleines Geschenk gegeben wird.

Übung	**10-2**

*Rewrite each passive-voice clause in the active voice, using **man** as the subject.*

1. Es ist oft gesagt worden ...

   _____

2. Die alte Frau wurde betrogen ...

   _____

3. Sie werden davor gewarnt werden ...

   _____

4. Es wird manchmal geschrieben ...

   _____

5. Es wird gehofft ...

   _____

Relative Pronouns

A relative pronoun is a word that reflects back to an antecedent in one sentence and connects that sentence with another sentence, combining the two sentences into one. The English relative pronouns are *that, who,* and *which.*

> *The story is true. I'm going to tell you the story.*
> *The story **that** I'm going to tell you is true.*
>
> *The mayor is quite popular. The mayor happens to be in Spain.*
> *The mayor, **who** happens to be in Spain, is quite popular.*
>
> *The medicine is strong. The medicine is now available over the counter.*
> *The medicine, **which** is now available over the counter, is strong.*

But English also has an elliptical relative construction, which omits the pronoun from the relative clause.

With the pronoun   *The boy **that** I saw had red hair.*
Without the pronoun   *The boy I saw had red hair.*

Der/die/das

German generally replaces each of these types of English relative pronouns with a definite article that serves as a relative pronoun. The declension of the definite article used as a relative pronoun is identical to the declension of the definite article alone, with the exception of the genitive case and the dative plural.

	Masculine	Feminine	Neuter	Plural
Nominative	der	die	das	die
Accusative	den	die	das	die
Dative	dem	der	dem	**denen**
Genitive	**dessen**	**deren**	**dessen**	**deren**

Although the German relative pronoun looks like a definite article, its meaning is *that, who,* or *which.* In its use as a relative pronoun, the definite article retains the gender, number, and case of the noun replaced in the relative clause.

When two German sentences share the same noun, one of the nouns can be changed to a relative pronoun and the two sentences can be combined into one.

> Erich besuchte **eine Tante. Eine Tante** wohnt in Heidelberg.
> Erich besuchte **eine Tante, die** in Heidelberg wohnt.
> *Erich visited an aunt who lives in Heidelberg.*

Notice that the relative pronoun **die** has the same gender, number, and case as the noun, **eine Tante**, that it replaces. In the relative clause, the conjugated verb **wohnt** is the last element in the clause. This occurs in all relative clauses, which are subordinate clauses and require the conjugated verb at the end.

As the gender, number, and case of a noun replaced by a relative pronoun changes, so, too, must the relative pronoun change.

Nominative masculine singular
_____

Heinz will einen Wagen, **der** neuer ist.
Heinz wants a car that is newer.

Accusative feminine singular
_____

Wir treffen die Dame, **die** meine Mutter kennt.
We meet the lady that my mother knows.

Dative neuter singular
_____

Er sucht das Mädchen, **mit dem** er getanzt hat.
He's looking for the girl he danced with.

Genitive plural
_____

Ich helfe den Touristen, **deren** Verwandte hier in der Stadt wohnen.
I help the tourists whose relatives live here in the city.

In the example for the dative neuter singular, notice that the German preposition **mit** stands directly in front of the relative pronoun **dem**. Although English is more flexible about the position of a preposition in a relative clause, the German preposition always stands in front of the relative pronoun.

> *. . . the girl with whom he danced.*
> *. . . the girl that he danced with.* } ... das Mädchen, **mit dem** er getanzt hat.
> *. . . the girl he danced with.*

Whatever the position of the English preposition, the German preposition has only one place in the relative clause.

> Hier ist der Kleiderschrank, **in dem** meine Anzüge aufbewahrt sind.
> *Here's the wardrobe that my suits are kept in.*

> In der Ferne ist der Tunnel, **durch den** der Zug fahren wird.
> *In the distance is the tunnel that the train will travel through.*

> Das ist ein Bild von meinen Söhnen, **von denen** ich heute diese Blumen
>   bekommen habe.
> *This is a picture of my sons, from whom I received these flowers today.*

The genitive of the relative pronoun replaces a possessive modifier or the genitive case of a noun.

Kennst du den Mann? Seine Frau ist gestern gestorben.
Kennst du den Mann, **dessen** Frau gestern gestorben ist?
Do you know the man whose wife died yesterday?

Werner besuchte die Schauspielerin. Ihr Talent ist weltberühmt.
Werner besuchte die Schauspielerin, **deren** Talent weltberühmt ist.
Werner visited the actress whose talent is world famous.

Sie helfen den Touristen. Ihre Pässe sind ungültig.
Sie helfen den Touristen, **deren** Pässe ungültig sind.
They help the tourists whose passports are invalid.

In sentences where a possessive relative pronoun is used, the modified noun remains in the sentence (in the sentences above, **dessen** *Frau,* **deren** *Talent,* **deren** *Pässe*). Because the possessive relative pronoun reflects back to the antecedent in the first sentence, it must have the gender and number of that antecedent. The noun that is modified does not affect the form of the possessive relative pronoun.

Kennst du den Mann, **dessen** Frau gestern gestorben ist?
(**dessen** replaces **seine**, which refers to **Mann**)

In the sentence above, the word **Frau** could be replaced by other nouns of different genders and number and the sentence would remain structured in the same way.

Kennst du den Mann, **dessen** Vater gestern gestorben ist?
Do you know the man whose father died yesterday?

Kennst du den Mann, **dessen** Kind gestern gestorben ist?
Do you know the man whose child died yesterday?

Kennst du den Mann, **dessen** Schwester gestern gestorben ist?
Do you know the man whose sister died yesterday?

Kennst du den Mann, **dessen** Freunde gestern gestorben sind?
Do you know the man whose friends died yesterday?

The noun that **dessen** modifies does not determine the gender or number of the relative pronoun—the antecedent **Mann** does. If the antecedent changes, the possessive relative pronoun may also change.

Kennst du **die Frau**, **deren** Vater gestern gestorben ist?
Do you know the woman whose father died yesterday?

Kennst du **das Kind**, **dessen** Vater gestern gestorben ist?
Do you know the child whose father died yesterday?

Kennst du **den Arzt**, **dessen** Vater gestern gestorben ist?
Do you know the physician whose father died yesterday?

Kennst du **die Kinder**, **deren** Vater gestern gestorben ist?
Do you know the children whose father died yesterday?

The genitive relative pronoun may also be used to replace a genitive noun.

Kennst du den Mann? Die Frau **des Mannes** ist gestern gestorben.
Kennst du den Mann, **dessen** Frau gestern gestorben ist?
Do you know the man whose wife died yesterday?

Wo sind die Blumen? Der Geruch **der Blumen** ist so schön.
Wo sind die Blumen, **deren** Geruch so schön ist?
Where are the flowers whose scent (the scent of which) is so pretty?

Ich suche den Rechtsanwalt. Ich habe die Mappe **des Rechtsanwalts** gefunden.
Ich suche den Rechtsanwalt, **dessen** Mappe ich gefunden habe.
I'm looking for the lawyer whose briefcase I found.

Sie kann der Lehrerin nicht antworten. Die Fragen **der Lehrerin** sind sehr schwierig.
Sie kann der Lehrerin, **deren** Fragen sehr schwierig sind, nicht antworten.
She can't answer the teacher whose questions are very hard.

Thus, both a possessive modifier and a genitive noun can be replaced in the very same way by a genitive relative pronoun.

Übung   **11-1**

Rewrite the relative clause in each sentence, taking into account each new antecedent.

1. Er findet ein Buch, das seinem Freund gehört.

   a. Er findet einen Handschuh, _____.

   b. Er findet eine Mappe, _____.

   c. Er findet die Anzüge, _____.

2. Ich sprach mit einem Freund, den Liese neulich kennen gelernt hat.

   a. Ich sprach mit einer Freundin, _____.

   b. Ich sprach mit dem Mädchen, _____.

   c. Ich sprach mit den Ausländern, _____.

3. Klaus kennt die Frau, von der die anderen gesprochen haben.

   a. Klaus kennt den Herrn, _____.

   b. Klaus kennt die Leute, _____.

   c. Klaus kennt das Kind, _____.

4. Sie besuchte die Dame, deren Nachbar aus England kommt.

   a. Sie besuchte ihre Verwandten, _____.

   b. Sie besuchte den Professor, _____.

   c. Sie besuchte die Krankenschwester, _____.

Welcher

Frequently, relative pronouns formed from definite articles are replaced by **welcher**. The endings for this form of the relative pronoun are the same as the ones used with **welcher** when it is a modifier, with the exception of the genitive case.

	Masculine	Feminine	Neuter	Plural
Nominative	welcher	welche	welches	welche
Accusative	welchen	welche	welches	welche
Dative	welchem	welcher	welchem	welchen
Genitive	**dessen**	**deren**	**dessen**	**deren**

Example phrases follow.

> der Hund, der stundenlang bellt OR der Hund, welcher stundenlang bellt
> *the dog that barks for hours*

> das Haus, das weiß ist OR das Haus, welches weiß ist
> *the house that's white*

> die Bücher, die er liest OR die Bücher, welche er liest
> *the books that he reads*

Like **der/die/das** used as a relative pronoun, **welcher** retains the gender, number, and case of the noun it replaces in a relative clause. When **welcher** is the relative pronoun in a clause, the conjugated verb is still the last element in the clause.

> Der Schüler, welcher nichts **lernt**, ist faul.
> *The pupil who isn't learning anything is lazy.*

In German, relative clauses are separated from the rest of the sentence by commas; this is not necessarily so in English, where the presence or absence of commas typically impacts the meaning of the sentence.

Übung   11-2

Rewrite each sentence, changing the definite article used as a relative pronoun to the appropriate form of **welcher**.

1. Der Tourist, mit dem er gesprochen hat, war Ausländer.

   _____

2. Der Schriftsteller, dessen Romane viel bewundert werden, ist jetzt achtzig Jahre alt.

   _____

3. Sie haben Beethoven ein Denkmal gesetzt, das ein junger Bildhauer geschaffen hat.

   _____

4. Sie kauft neue Gläser, aus denen man nur Wein trinken wird.

_____

5. Der Zug, der langsam fährt, ist kein Eilzug.

_____

Was

In certain cases, **was** is used as a relative pronoun. This occurs when the antecedent of the relative pronoun is **alles**, **etwas**, **nichts**, or **viel(es)**.

Ich verstehe **alles, was** Sie sagen.
I understand everything you're saying.

Sie kaufte **etwas, was** wirklich zu teuer war.
She bought something that was really too expensive.

Hans lernt **nichts, was** gelehrt wird.
Hans isn't learning anything that is being taught.

Es gibt **viel(es), was** dem Körper schaden kann.
There's a lot that can harm the body.

In addition, when **das** is used as a demonstrative pronoun, **was** is used as the relative pronoun.

Ich lese ein bisschen von **dem, was** er geschrieben hat.
I read a little of what he wrote.

When an adjective is used as a neuter noun, **was** is used as the relative pronoun.

Ich brauche **das Beste, was** Sie haben.
I need the best that you have.

Was is also used as a relative pronoun when the antecedent of the relative clause is an entire clause.

Sie fing an zu weinen, was ihn sehr überrascht hat.
She started to cry, which really surprised him.

When **was** is the subject (as, for instance, in **... was dem Körper schaden kann** above) or direct object (as in **... was er geschrieben hat** above) of a relative clause, it does not make a declensional change. When **was** is the object of a preposition, a form like a prepositional adverb is used: **wo(r)-** + preposition.

In zwei Tagen fängt Fasching an, **worauf** ich mich sehr freue.
Fasching starts in two days, which I'm really looking forward to.

Sie verkaufte alles, **womit** sie nach Berlin gezogen war.
She sold everything she moved to Berlin with.

Prepositional adverbs will be treated in detail in Unit 18.

The interrogatives **wer** and **was** are used as special relative pronouns, where in English _whoever/whosoever_ or _whatever/whatsoever_ is used. In some instances, these two pronouns can be translated simply as *who* or *what*. **Wer** or **was** begins the first clause, and **der** or **das** is used in the second clause, although **der** and **das** can sometimes be omitted.

> **Wer** nicht lernen will, **dem** wird nichts gelingen.
> *Whoever does not want to learn will succeed at nothing.*

> **Was** du findest, **das** gehört jetzt dir.
> *What you find now belongs to you.*

Wer in this usage can be declined in all cases.

Nominative	**wer**
Accusative	**wen**
Dative	**wem**
Genitive	**wessen** (**Wessen** is sometimes pronounced as **wes**.)

Example sentences follow.

> Wer ihn trifft, (der) vergisst ihn nie.
> *Whoever meets him never forgets him.*

> Wen man befreit, den befreundet man.
> *Whomever you free you make your friend.*

> Wem man nicht traut, dem bleibt man fern.
> *Stay away from whomever you don't trust.*

> Wessen Brot wird gegessen, dessen Lied wird gesungen.
> *Whoever's bread is eaten, his song will be sung.*

Übung   11-3

Fill in each blank with the appropriate relative pronoun.

1. Die Zeitung, von _____ der Held gelobt wurde, war das Abendblatt.

2. Die Uhr, _____ an der Wand hängt, war ein Geschenk von meiner Mutter.

3. Mein Mann gibt mir alles, _____ ich verlange.

4. _____ nicht mein Freund ist, der ist mein Feind.

5. Ich kaufte einen schweren Mantel, _____ ich im Winter tragen werde.

6. Das große Haus, _____ an der Ecke gebaut wird, ist furchtbar teuer.

7. Ich brauche einen Schrank, in _____ ich mein Geld aufbewahren kann.

8. Sie sucht ein Thermometer, mit _____ sie das Fieber ihres Sohnes messen kann.

9. Das ist der Lehrer, _____ Schüler durchgefallen sind.

10. Siehst du den Wagen, _____ ich gestern gekauft habe?

Übung | 11-4

Complete each sentence with any appropriate relative clause.

1. Am Himmel sehe ich die Sterne, ⸺⸺⸺⸺⸺⸺⸺⸺⸺ .

2. Er gab mir etwas, ⸺⸺⸺⸺⸺⸺⸺⸺⸺ .

3. Das sind die Soldaten, von denen ⸺⸺⸺⸺⸺⸺⸺⸺⸺ .

4. Er kaufte sich einen Schlips, ⸺⸺⸺⸺⸺⸺⸺⸺⸺ .

5. Ich lese nichts, wofür ⸺⸺⸺⸺⸺⸺⸺⸺⸺ .

Reflexive Pronouns

English reflexive pronouns, which end in -self (singular) and -selves (plural), are the reflexive counterparts of subject pronouns.

Personal pronoun	Reflexive pronoun
I	myself
you	yourself
he	himself
she	herself
it	itself
we	ourselves
you	yourselves
they	themselves

German does not use a suffix to form reflexive pronouns. Instead, the accusative or dative form of the personal pronoun—except for the third-person singular and plural forms—is used as the reflexive form. Just as in English, German reflexive pronouns are the counterparts of subject pronouns.

Nominative	Accusative reflexive	Dative reflexive
ich	mich	mir
du	dich	dir
er	**sich**	**sich**
sie	**sich**	**sich**
es	**sich**	**sich**
wir	uns	uns
ihr	euch	euch
sie	**sich**	**sich**
Sie	**sich**	**sich**
man	sich	sich
wer	**sich**	**sich**
was	**sich**	**sich**

Since singular and plural nouns are in the third person, their reflexive pronoun form is always **sich**.

The accusative reflexive pronoun is used to replace the accusative object of a verb. When the object of the verb is *not* the same person or thing as the subject of the sentence, a reflexive pronoun is not used.

> Karl ärgert **seinen Vater**.
> *Karl annoys his father.*

> Was fragst du **ihn**?
> *What are you asking him?*

> Helga schützt **sie** davor.
> *Helga protects her from it.*

But when the object of the verb is the same person or thing as the subject, the reflexive counterpart of the subject is used.

> Karl ärgert **sich**.
> *Karl annoys himself. / Karl is annoyed.*

> Was fragst du **dich**?
> *What are you asking yourself?*

> Helga schützt **sich** davor.
> *Helga protects herself from it.*

Übung 12-1

Rewrite each sentence, changing the direct object in boldface to the appropriate reflexive pronoun.

1. Ich möchte **meine Freundin** vorstellen.

   _____

2. Wir haben **den Professor** wieder geärgert.

   _____

3. Du musst **die Kinder** vor einer Erkältung schützen.

   _____

4. Habt ihr **die Kinder** angekleidet?

   _____

5. Wie können sie **die Lage** ändern?

   _____

6. Meine Mutter fragt **meinen Vater**, was geschehen ist.

   _____

7. Frau Schneider hat **die Katze** auf einen Stuhl gesetzt.

   _____

8. Du hast **mich** schon überzeugt.

   _____

9. Der wahnsinnige Mann hat **sie** getötet.

   _____

10. Ich wasche **ihn.**

    _____

When the object of a verb is not the same person or thing as the subject of the sentence, a reflexive pronoun is not used.

> Wir trauen **dir** diese Arbeit zu.
> _We entrust you with this job._

> Ich kaufe **dem Kind** eine Blume.
> _I buy the child a flower._

> Er bestellt **ihr** eine Tasse Tee.
> _He orders her a cup of tea._

But when the dative object of the verb is the same person or thing as the subject, the dative reflexive counterpart of the subject is used.

> Wir trauen **uns** diese Arbeit zu.
> _We entrust ourselves with this job._

> Ich kaufe **mir** eine Blume.
> _I buy myself a flower._

> Er bestellt **sich** eine Tasse Tee.
> _He orders himself a cup of tea._

The accusative case is used for direct objects and after prepositions that take the accusative case. An accusative reflexive pronoun is used in these two instances just as a noun or a personal pronoun is.

> Ich freue mich auf die Ferien.
> _I'm looking forward to vacation._

> Er hat es nur für sich getan.
> _He has only done it for himself._

The dative case is used for indirect objects, with dative verbs, and after dative prepositions. A dative reflexive pronoun is used in these three instances just as a noun or a personal pronoun is.

> Er findet sich einen neuen Schlips.
> _He finds a new tie for himself._

> Sie helfen sich, so gut sie können.
> _They help themselves as well as they can._

> Ich habe kein Geld bei mir.
> _I don't have any money on me._

Übung 12-2

Rewrite each sentence, changing the dative object in boldface to the appropriate reflexive pronoun.

1. Die Mutter putzt **dem kleinsten Kind** die Zähne.

   _____

2. Gudrun hilft **den anderen**, so gut sie kann.

   _____

3. Martin und Erich wollen **uns** ein Spiel kaufen.

   _____

4. Warum musst du **dem Lehrer** widersprechen?

   _____

5. Ich kämme **ihm** die Haare.

   _____

6. Darf ich **meinem Freund** ein Stück Kuchen nehmen?

   _____

7. Meine Schwester hat **mir** ein interessantes Buch gefunden.

   _____

8. Er kaufte **seinem besten Freund** eine Armbanduhr.

   _____

9. Das wird sie **Ihnen** nie verzeihen.

   _____

10. Habt ihr **den Kindern** die Mäntel ausgezogen?

    _____

Übung 12-3

Rewrite each sentence, changing the accusative or dative object in boldface to the appropriate reflexive pronoun.

1. Was hat **es** bewegt?

   _____

2. Ich kann **diesen armen Leuten** nicht helfen.

_____

3. Haben Sie **Ihrem Mann** nicht widersprochen?

_____

4. Wir haben **den jungen Kandidaten** vorgestellt.

_____

5. Wer hat **sie** gewaschen?

_____

6. Sie hat **ihren Mann** an die Italienreise erinnert.

_____

7. Man soll **den Manager** nicht ärgern.

_____

8. Herr Finkler hat **seinem einzigen Sohn** einen neuen Wagen gekauft.

_____

9. Sie haben **uns** ein paar Pralinen genommen.

_____

10. Du musst **sie** ändern.

_____

In order to achieve a specific meaning, some verbs require a reflexive pronoun to act as part of the verb. If the reflexive pronoun is omitted, the meaning is changed. These are called reflexive verbs and are identified as such in dictionaries, because the addition of a reflexive pronoun is important to the meaning of the verb. Examples of the range of meaning and use of the verb **vorstellen** follow.

> Ich kann ihn vorstellen.
> _I can introduce him._

In this example, **vorstellen** is not a reflexive verb; it is a transitive verb with a direct object (**ihn**).

> Ich kann mich vorstellen.
> _I can introduce myself._

In this example, **vorstellen** is also not a reflexive verb; it is a transitive verb with a reflexive direct object (**mich**). It is not a reflexive verb, because the meaning remains the same whether the direct object is a reflexive pronoun or some other word.

> Ich kann mir das vorstellen.
> _I can imagine that._

In this example, the verb **sich vorstellen** is a dative reflexive verb that means *to imagine*. This meaning is achieved only if the reflexive pronoun remains part of the verb. If the subject changes, the reflexive pronoun must change accordingly.

> Du kannst dir das vorstellen.
> *You can imagine that.*

> Er kann sich das vorstellen.
> *He can imagine that.*

> Sie kann sich das vorstellen.
> *She can imagine that.*

> Wir können uns das vorstellen.
> *We can imagine that.*

Following is a list of other reflexive verbs that require a reflexive pronoun to act together with the verb to achieve a desired meaning.

sich einbilden (*dative reflexive*)	*to imagine something*
sich erkälten (*accusative reflexive*)	*to catch cold*
sich irren (*accusative reflexive*)	*to be wrong*
sich vornehmen (*dative reflexive*)	*to intend to do something*

German has numerous other reflexive verbs. To be certain that a reflexive pronoun is required to achieve a particular meaning, check the dictionary entry for the verb. For example, the entry for the verb **benehmen** may appear as follows.

benehmen 1. *ir.v.a.* take away. 2. *v.r.* behave, demean oneself.

Definition 1 identifies **benehmen** as an **ir**regular **v**erb and transitive (that is, **a**ctive), meaning *take away*. Definition 2 identifies it as a **v**erb that is **r**eflexive, meaning *to behave* or *demean oneself*. This two-letter abbreviation (**v.r.**) tells you that this verb is reflexive and achieves its meaning by acting together with a reflexive pronoun in its conjugation.

ich benehme mich	*I behave myself*
du benimmst dich	*you behave yourself*
er benahm sich	*he behaved himself*
sie hat sich benommen	*she has behaved herself*
wir hatten uns benommen	*we had behaved ourselves*
sie werden sich benehmen	*they will behave themselves*

Verbs that have to do with getting dressed require special consideration. Three high-frequency verbs are derived from the infinitive **ziehen** and combined with prefixes that change the basic meaning of the verb.

anziehen	*to put on (clothes)*
ausziehen	*to take off (clothes)*
umziehen	*to change (clothes)*

These three verbs can be used with a direct object. The meaning is that someone is putting on, taking off, or changing certain clothing.

> Ich möchte den neuen Regenmantel anziehen.
> *I'd like to put on the new raincoat.*

> Die nassen Kinder zogen ihre Hemden aus.
> *The wet children took off their shirts.*

Der schwitzende Läufer zieht die Schuhe um.
The sweating runner changes shoes.

The same verbs can be used with an accusative reflexive pronoun to refer to dressing in general, with no particular article of clothing specified.

Nach einer langen Dusche habe ich mich angezogen.
After a long shower I got dressed.

Der schüchterne Junge will sich nicht ausziehen.
The shy boy doesn't want to undress.

Kannst du dich nicht schneller umziehen?
Can't you change faster?

Finally, these verbs can be used with an indirect object in the form of a dative reflexive pronoun. In addition, the sentence also contains a direct object (an article of clothing).

Sie möchte sich ein blaues Kleid anziehen.
She'd like to put on a blue dress.

Willst du dir den schweren Mantel ausziehen?
Do you want to take off the heavy coat?

Er hat sich die Stiefel umziehen wollen.
He wanted to change his boots.

Übung	12-4

Rewrite each sentence, using the subjects in parentheses and changing the accusative or dative object in boldface to the appropriate reflexive pronoun. Be sure to make any necessary changes to the verb.

1. Seine Freundin denkt nur an **ihn**.

   a. (ich)   _____

   b. (du)   _____

   c. (die Kinder) _____

   d. (Sie)   _____

2. Gerda kaufte **mir** neue Handschuhe.

   a. (ich)   _____

   b. (er)   _____

   c. (wir)   _____

   d. (du)   _____

3. Wir brauchen Hustentropfen für **unsere Tochter**.

    a. (der alte Mann)   _____

    b. (sie [*sing.*])   _____

    c. (ihr)   _____

    d. (Erich)   _____

Übung   **12-5**

Rewrite each sentence, changing the reflexive pronoun to any appropriate noun or noun phrase.

1. Wir werden uns diese Arbeit zutrauen.

_____

2. Braucht ihr das Geld für euch?

_____

3. Ich kann mich nicht davon überzeugen.

_____

4. Sie dürfen sich auf diese Bank setzen.

_____

5. Marianne stellte sich neben ihren Vater.

_____

6. Meine Eltern haben sich einen bunten Teppich gekauft.

_____

7. Er fragt sich, ob das eine Dummheit ist.

_____

8. Du sollst dich sofort vorstellen.

_____

9. Karl hat sich einen guten Platz gesucht.

_____

10. Ich ziehe mir das Hemd an.

_____

Übung 12-6

Circle the pronoun that best completes each sentence.

1. Ich habe das Geld für _____ gebraucht.   ihm | sich | mich

2. Wie hast du _____ wieder erkältet?   dich | ihr | dir

3. Karl möchte _____ ein neues Fahrrad kaufen.   sich | ihn | es

4. Das werden Sie _____ nie verzeihen.   mich | euch | sich

5. Darf ich _____ vorstellen?   euch | sich | du

6. Bitte setzen Sie _____!   uns | sich | ihm

7. Martin will _____ den Pullover ausziehen.   mich | dich | sich

8. Wo kann ich _____ die Hände waschen?   sich | uns | mir

9. Hast du _____ wieder umgezogen?   dir | dich | Ihnen

10. Er hat _____ diese Arbeit zugetraut.   mir | Sie | ihn

Reciprocal Pronouns

English has two reciprocal pronouns: *each other* and *one another.* Both are translated into German as **einander**. This pronoun is never used as the subject of a sentence. Its use is similar to that of the reflexive pronoun, but it always refers back to two or more persons or things in a plural antecedent. The following examples show the basic English and German constructions.

> *Maria helps Tom. Tom helps Maria.* →
> *Maria and Tom help **one another**.*
>   OR *Maria and Tom help **each other**.*

> Maria hilft Thomas. Thomas hilft Maria. →
> Maria und Thomas helfen **einander**.

In the German example, **Maria und Thomas** is the plural antecedent, and **einander** is the object of the dative verb **helfen**. **Einander** does not decline; there is no difference in the form of this pronoun whether it is accusative or dative.

> Die alten Klassenkameraden haben **einander** vergessen.
>   (accusative direct object)
> *The old classmates have forgotten one another.*

> Die Sieger wollen **einander** gratulieren.
>   (object of dative verb)
> *The winners want to congratulate each other.*

When used with prepositions, **einander** makes no declensional changes, but it is written with the preposition as one word.

miteinander
voneinander
zueinander

> Die Freunde haben oft **aneinander** gedacht.
> *The friends often thought about one another.*

> Die zwei Armeen kämpften tagelang **gegeneinander**.
> *The two armies battled against one another for days.*

> Sie legte die neulich gestrickten Pullover **nebeneinander**.
> *She laid the recently knitted sweaters next to one another.*

Notice in these examples that the plural antecedents of **aneinander** and **gegeneinander** are the subjects of the sentence: **Die Freunde** and **Die zwei Armeen**. But in the third example with **nebeneinander**, the plural antecedent is the direct object: **die neulich gestrickten Pullover**. Although the antecedent of **einander** is always plural, it can be in any of the four cases.

Übung	13-1

Rewrite each sentence or pair of sentences as one sentence, using the pronoun **einander**.

EXAMPLE   Er hilft ihr. Sie hilft ihm.

Sie helfen einander.

1. Erich schickt Klaus ein paar Briefe. Klaus schickt Erich ein paar Briefe.

2. Der eine Ausländer versteht nicht den anderen.

3. Die eine Schwester kaufte der anderen Geschenke.

4. Der eine Reisende wollte mit dem anderen sprechen.

5. Ich besuchte sie. Sie besuchte mich.

6. Der eine Tennisspieler spielte sehr schlecht gegen den anderen.

7. Die Jungen beobachten die Mädchen. Die Mädchen beobachten die Jungen.

8. Oma sorgt um Opa. Opa sorgt um Oma.

9. Karl hat nach Klaudia gefragt. Klaudia hat nach Karl gefragt.

10. Er stellt die eine Vase neben die andere.

Übung	13-2

Write original sentences, using the pronouns in parentheses.

1. (einander)

   _____

2. (miteinander)

   _____

3. (füreinander)

   _____

4. (gegeneinander)

   _____

5. (voneinander)

   _____

PART II

PREPOSITIONS

Prepositions are words that show the relationship between nouns/pronouns and other elements of a sentence. They describe time, place, manner, or direction.

*the color **of** the ceiling*   (***of*** tells whose color)
*a room **in** the attic*   (***in*** describes a location)
*a gift **from** me*   (***from*** describes the source)

German prepositions have the same function, and because they require the use of a specific case (accusative, dative, or genitive), there are nuances of meaning to be considered. The following examples show how case affects the meaning of a preposition.

| Accusative case | Er wartet **auf den** Mann. |
| | *He waits for the man.* |

| Dative case | Was liegt **auf dem** Mann? |
| | *What's lying on the man?* |

In the first example (***auf den** Mann*), the noun object is in the accusative case and the preposition is translated as *for*. In the second example (***auf dem** Mann*), the noun object is in the dative case and the preposition indicates location *on the man*. The meaning of the phrase is altered by the change of the case from accusative to dative.

A large part of this section is devoted to how prepositions function in order to form other parts of speech. This is achieved principally by using prepositions as prefixes to nouns, verbs, adjectives, and adverbs.

The preposition **aus**

Used as a dative preposition	**aus** dem Garten	*out of the garden*
Used to form a noun	die **Aus**nahme	*the exception*
Used to form an adjective	**aus**führlich	*in detail*

This section guides you through the maze of prepositional types and uses and clarifies their function in a sentence. They will be described and illustrated for you, and then you will have ample opportunity to practice with them in the exercises.

By increasing your ability to use prepositions effectively and accurately, you will bring your German skills to a higher level.

Accusative Prepositions

English nouns do not decline when they are used as direct objects or in prepositional phrases. In German, however, direct objects and objects of accusative prepositions are functions of the accusative case, and masculine nouns make declensional changes in this case.

	Nominative case	Accusative case
Masculine	der Vater	**den** Vater
Feminine	die Frau	die Frau
Neuter	das Kind	das Kind
Plural	die Lampen	die Lampen

The following are the most common accusative prepositions, and masculine nouns in phrases with these prepositions must appear in the accusative case. Remember: Feminine, neuter, and plural nouns do not decline in the accusative case.

bis	*until, up to*	gegen	*against*
durch	*through*	ohne	*without*
entlang	*along, down*	um	*around, about*
für	*for*	wider	*against, contrary to*

In the following examples, notice how nouns appear in accusative prepositional phrases and how the masculine definite article changes.

Ich habe etwas für **den Mann**.
I have something for the man.

Er bittet um **die Adresse**.
He asks for the address.

Sie laufen durch **das Haus**.
They run through the house.

Er kommt ohne **die Kinder**.
He comes without the children.

Unlike the other accusative prepositions, the preposition **entlang** follows its noun object.

> Der Weg führte den Fluss **entlang**.
> *The path went along the river.*

When accusative prepositions are used with pronouns that refer to *animate* nouns, the prepositional phrase consists of preposition + accusative pronoun.

> Es ist ein Geschenk **für dich**.
> *It's a gift for you.*

> Kommst du **ohne ihn**?
> *Are you coming without him?*

> Ich denke er ist **gegen mich**.
> *I think he's against me.*

If you ask the question *whom* with an accusative preposition, the nominative **wer** changes to the accusative **wen**.

> Das ist ein Geschenk für meinen Bruder.
> **Für wen** ist das Geschenk?
> *Whom is the gift for?*

> Er hat gegen den Dieb gesprochen.
> **Gegen wen** hat er gesprochen?
> *Whom did he speak against?*

> Die Touristen stehen um den Reiseleiter.
> **Um wen** stehen die Touristen?
> *Whom are the tourists standing around?*

Übung   14-1

Rewrite each sentence, using the appropriate form of the word or phrase in parentheses to fill in the blank.

1. Eine Fledermaus ist durch _____ geflogen.

   a. (das Haus)   _____

   b. (die Scheune)   _____

   c. (der große Lesesaal) _____

   d. (unsere Schule)   _____

2. Warum ist er gegen _____?

   a. (seine Kinder)   _____

   b. (sein Sohn)   _____

   c. (ihr älterer Bruder) _____

   d. (seine Tante)   _____

3. Der neue Manager handelte ohne _____.

    a. (jede Rücksicht auf uns) _____

    b. (Vernunft) _____

    c. (Überlegung) _____

4. Ich möchte bis _____ bleiben.

    a. (Freitag) _____

    b. (nächster Samstag) _____

    c. (morgen) _____

5. Welcher Weg führt _____ entlang?

    a. (der schöne Bach) _____

    b. (dieser Wald) _____

    c. (jener Zaun) _____

    d. (kein Fluss) _____

Übung 14-2

Fill in each blank with the appropriate preposition. Choose from **für,** **bis,** *and* **um.**

1. Ich habe mich immer _____ meine Familie bemüht.

2. Morgen fahren wir _____ Freiburg.

3. Darf ich _____ Ihren Vornamen bitten?

4. Erich hat _____ 40 Euro zwei alte Pullover verkauft.

5. Ich habe Onkel Heinz _____ das nette Geschenk gedankt.

6. Diese Arbeit ist typisch _____ einen achtjährigen.

7. Ich war oft _____ meine Eltern besorgt.

8. Ich werde mit dir _____ an das Ende der Straße gehen.

9. Kommen Sie _____ dreizehn Uhr?

10. Der Stadtgraben ging _____ die ganze Stadt.

Multiple Usages

The meaning of the accusative prepositions shown in the lists and examples above is their *basic meaning*. Accusative prepositions, however, have more than one use and therefore have to be translated into English appropriately to achieve the intended meaning.

Bis

Bis is generally used to show movement toward a goal, and that goal can be a location, an amount, or a point in time. When used with locations, it often means *as far as* or *up to*.

bis Berlin	*as far as Berlin*
bis hier	*up to here*

With amounts, it means *up to* or *as much as*.

bis 100 Euro	*as much as 100 euros*
bis 10 Liter	*up to ten liters*

Notice that no article is used in the expressions above. However, when an article is used, a second preposition tends to accompany **bis**.

Wir gingen bis **zum** Irrgarten.
We went as far as the maze.

Sie fliegen bis **über** die Wolken.
They're flying up over the clouds.

Er bleibt hier bis **nach** den Ferien.
He's staying here until after vacation.

In these examples, the translation of **bis** varies, although the general idea of *up to, until,* or *as far as* is still expressed in some form to show movement toward a goal.

Durch

Durch means *through* or *across* and identifies movement through a certain space.

Wir laufen durch den Wald.
We run through the woods.

Ich schwimme durch den Fluss.
I swim across the river.

But when **durch** is used to express movement across time, the meaning changes slightly.

Wir lebten den Herbst durch in Wien.
We lived through the fall in Vienna.

Es geschieht durch die Geschichte.
It occurs throughout history.

Notice that the preposition **durch** in the expression **den Herbst durch** follows its object.

In the passive voice, **durch** is used to indicate the cause of an action.

Der Mann ist durch einen Unfall getötet worden.
The man was killed due to an accident.

Durch also describes the *means* by which an action is carried out.

> Wir werden die Geschenke durch die Post schicken.
> *We'll send the gifts by mail.*

Für

Für means *for* and signifies that something is being done for the benefit of someone or something. In this meaning, it is the opposite of **gegen** (*against*).

> Luise arbeitet für ihre Familie.
> *Luise works for her family.*

> Ich kämpfe für ein besseres Leben.
> *I struggle for a better life.*

Für can also signify a replacement for someone or something else.

> Der Freund schreibt die Briefe für seinen kranken Kameraden.
> *The friend writes the letters for his sick pal.*

Für is also used to express an amount of money or a price.

> Ich arbeite nur für Geld.
> *I'm just working for the money.*

> Sie kauft für 5 Euro einen Schlips.
> *She buys a tie for 5 euros.*

Gegen

Gegen has the basic meaning *against*. It is the opposite of **für**.

> Warum kämpfen sie immer gegeneinander?
> *Why are they always fighting against one another?*

> Die Jungen sind gegen den Strom geschwommen.
> *The boys swam against the current.*

Gegen also means *approximately* or *toward* in expressions of time or amount.

> Sie sind gegen 23 Uhr angekommen.
> *They arrived toward 11 P.M.*

> Mein Urgroßvater ist jetzt gegen 90 Jahre alt.
> *My great-grandfather is almost 90 years old now.*

Ohne

Ohne indicates that someone or something is *not present*. Its general meaning is *without*.

> Der arme Mann ist jetzt ohne Wohnung.
> *The poor man is now without an apartment.*

> Das junge Ehepaar ist noch ohne Kinder.
> *The young couple is still without children.*

Um

Um is used to express the time as shown on a clock.

> Es ist um Mitternacht geschehen.
> *It happened at midnight.*

> Ich komme um 10 Uhr nach Hause.
> *I'll come home at 10 o'clock.*

This preposition is also frequently used to mean *around* and implies a circular motion around a person or object.

> Die Planeten bewegen sich endlos um die Sonne.
> *The planets move endlessly around the sun.*

Um is also used with certain verbs to achieve a specific meaning, and in such instances **um** can have a variety of translations.

er bemüht sich um	*he acts on behalf of*
ich bitte um	*I ask for*
wir weinen um	*we cry about*
sie kümmert sich um	*she cares about/for*

Wider

Wider, like **gegen**, is the opposite of **für**. It means *against* or *contrary to,* but is used less often than **gegen** and is found most frequently in poetic language.

> Der Chef handelte wider alle Vernunft.
> *The boss acted against all reason.*

Der-Words

Der-words are demonstratives that replace definite articles. They identify the gender of a noun like definite articles and decline in the same way. The **der**-words are **dieser** (*this*), **jener** (*that*), **jeder** (*each*), **solcher** (*such*), and **welcher** (*which*). Gender is shown in the nominative case of **der**-words and singular adjectives that follow end in **-e**.

	dieser	jener	jeder
Masculine	dieser gute Mann	jener gute Mann	jeder gute Mann
Feminine	diese nette Frau	jene nette Frau	jede nette Frau
Neuter	dieses alte Haus	jenes alte Haus	jedes alte Haus
Plural	diese guten Kinder	jene guten Kinder	—

Notice that **jeder** (*each*) is used only in the singular.

Following an accusative preposition, a masculine **der**-word declines like the definite article, and the ending of an adjective that follows becomes **-en**.

für **dies**en neu**en** Lehrer	*for this new teacher*
bis **jen**en froh**en** Tag	*until that happy day*

um jed**en** schön**en** Garten   *around each beautiful garden*
durch welch**en** alt**en** Bahnhof   *through which old railway station*

Ein-Words

Ein-words are demonstratives that replace indefinite articles. They are the possessive pronouns (**mein**, **dein**, **sein**, **ihr**, **unser**, **euer**, **ihr**, **Ihr**) and **kein** (*no, not any*). With **ein**-words, gender is shown in the adjective.

Masculine	Feminine	Neuter	Plural
mein alt**er** Mantel	deine neu**e** Mappe	mein rot**es** Buch	deine guten Kinder
sein alt**er** Wagen	ihre neu**e** Lampe	sein rot**es** Auto	ihre guten Kinder
unser alt**er** Onkel	eure neu**e** Schule	Ihr rot**es** Hemd	unsere guten Kinder
kein alt**er** Mann	keine neu**e** Tasse	kein rot**es** Dach	keine guten Kinder

Following an accusative preposition, a masculine **ein**-word declines like the indefinite article, and the ending of an adjective that follows becomes **-en**.

um mein**en** rot**en** Mantel   *around my red coat*
für dein**en** nett**en** Bruder   *for your nice brother*
durch Ihr**en** schön**en** Garten   *through your beautiful garden*
ohne unser**en** neu**en** Freund   *without our new friend*

Übung	14-3

Fill in each blank with any appropriate phrase.

1. Diese Leute haben viel für _____ getan.

2. Der blinde Mann stieß gegen _____ .

3. Gegen _____ sind wir endlich nach Hause gekommen.

4. Die Party fängt um _____ an.

5. Die Wanderer müssen durch _____ schwimmen.

6. Morgen reisen wir nur bis _____ .

7. Wir gingen bis zu _____ .

8. Mein Vater geht niemals ohne _____ aus dem Haus.

9. Ich habe es für _____ gekauft.

10. Die Mädchen gingen _____ entlang.

11. Der Polizist hat um _____ gebeten.

12. Die alte Scheune wurde durch _____ zerstört.

13. Wie kannst du das ohne _____ tun?

14. Warum ist Helmut gegen _____?

15. Sie hat sich selten um _____ gekümmert.

Dative Prepositions

The dative case is used to identify an indirect object or the object of a dative verb.

> Er gibt ihr einen Ring.
> *He gives her a ring.*

The indirect object is **ihr** in the example above.

> Sie helfen dem Mann.
> *She helps the man.*

In this example, the object of the dative verb **helfen** is **dem Mann**.

The dative case is also used after dative prepositions.

aus	*out, from*	nach	*after*
außer	*except (for)*	seit	*since*
bei	*at, by*	von	*from, of*
gegenüber	*opposite*	zu	*to, for*
mit	*with*		

Unlike the other dative prepositions, **gegenüber** usually follows its noun object.

> Dem Sofa **gegenüber** stand ein Tisch.
> *A table stood opposite the sofa.*

All nouns make a declensional change from the nominative to the dative, and this dative form is the one required following dative prepositions.

	Nominative	Dative
Masculine	der Mann	**dem** Mann
Feminine	die Frau	**der** Frau
Neuter	das Haus	**dem** Haus
Plural	die Kinder	**den** Kinder**n**

An adjective modifying a noun in the dative case always has an **-en** ending.

zu dem alt**en** Mann	*to the old man*
von dem groß**en** Haus	*from the big house*
mit der nett**en** Frau	*with the nice woman*
bei den klein**en** Kindern	*by the little children*

All **der**-words and **ein**-words have the same endings in the dative case. But as in other cases, **jeder** can only be used in the singular.

Masculine	Feminine	Neuter	Plural
zu dem Mann	mit der Frau	von dem Haus	bei den Kindern
zu diesem Mann	mit jener Frau	von jenem Haus	bei deinen Kindern
zu jedem Mann	mit seiner Frau	von ihrem Haus	bei solchen Kindern
zu keinem Mann	mit welcher Frau	von keinem Haus	bei Ihren Kindern

Examples of sentences with dative prepositions follow.

Der Vater sehnte sich nach **seinem ausgewanderten Sohn**.
The father longed for his emigrated son.

Ich habe diese Briefe von **deiner Frau** bekommen.
I received these letters from your wife.

Herr Bauer ist seit **dem ersten** Februar in Leipzig.
Mr. Bauer has been in Leipzig since the first of February.

Die amerikanischen Besucher möchten zu **ihren Verwandten** in Kiel reisen.
The American visitors would like to travel to their relatives in Kiel.

As with accusative prepositions, when dative prepositions are used with pronouns that refer to *animate* nouns, the prepositional phrase consists of preposition + dative pronoun.

Wir bekommen einen Brief **von ihm**.
We receive a letter from him.

Martin wohnt **bei ihnen**.
Martin lives at their house.

Haben Sie **mit ihr** gesprochen?
Did you speak with her?

If you ask the question *whom* with a dative preposition, the nominative **wer** changes to the dative **wem**.

Sie will mit Herrn Keller reden.
Mit wem will sie reden?
Whom does she want to talk with?

Wir gehen zu unseren Eltern.
Zu wem gehen wir?
Whose house are we going to?

Übung | **15-1**

Rewrite each sentence, using the appropriate form of the word or phrase in parentheses to fill in the blank.

1. Eine Fledermaus ist aus _____ geflogen.

   a. (das Haus) _____

   b. (die Kirche) _____

   c. (ein großes Fenster) _____

   d. (dieser Tunnel) _____

2. Wie lange wirst du bei _____ wohnen?

   a. (deine Tante) _____

   b. (diese Leute) _____

   c. (ein Bekannter) _____

   d. (dein Onkel) _____

3. Wir sind sehr zufrieden mit _____.

   a. (Ihre Arbeit) _____

   b. (diese Lösung) _____

   c. (einige Theorien) _____

   d. (der neue Angestellte) _____

4. Karl ist sehr unterschiedlich von _____.

   a. (sein Vater) _____

   b. (seine Geschwister) _____

   c. (seine Schwester) _____

   d. (seine Eltern) _____

Übung   15-2

Fill in the blank with the appropriate preposition. Choose from **aus**, **nach**, **von**, *and* **zu**.

1. Ich fahre morgen _____ Berlin.

2. Wir mussten den ganzen Tag _____ Hause bleiben.

3. Das ist eine Symphonie _____ Beethoven.

4. Der alte Mann hatte große Ähnlichkeit _____ meinem Großvater.

5. Der junge Student kommt jetzt _____ der Universität.

6. Früher baute man große Schiffe _____ Holz.

7. Diese Leute sind Verwandte _____ uns.

8. Othmarschen und Rahlstedt sind Vororte, die _____ Hamburg gehören.

9. Karin lief _____ dem Wohnzimmer und fing an zu weinen.

10. Die modernen Flugzeuge sind _____ Aluminium.

11. Ich wollte _____ dem Konzert in der Stadt bleiben.

12. _____ einer Minute kam die alte Dame an die Tür.

13. Martin fährt _____ einer Freundin in Kiel zu Besuch.

14. Wir werden jetzt eine Pause _____ 15 Minuten machen.

15. Sie hat den Brief _____ dem Englischen ins Deutsche übersetzt.

Multiple Usages

The meaning of the dative prepositions shown in the lists and examples above is their *basic meaning.*

Aus

Aus means *out* or *out of* and is generally used to show movement from an enclosed space or from an area surrounded by similar things. It is the opposite of **in**.

> Die Kinder laufen aus dem Haus.
> *The children run out of the house.*

Er zieht eine Münze aus der Tasche.
He takes a coin out of his pocket.

Aus means *from* when speaking or writing about cities and countries.

Meine deutschen Verwandten kommen aus Hamburg.
My German relatives come from Hamburg.

Kommen Sie aus Mexiko?
Do you come from Mexico?

Aus also means *from* when it refers to a point in time.

Diese komischen Ideen kommen aus alter Zeit.
These funny ideas come from the olden days.

It is also used to describe the reason for an action.

Sprechen Sie aus Erfahrung?
Are you speaking from experience?

Er hat seine Frau aus Ärger geschlagen.
He hit his wife out of anger.

Aus is also used to describe what something is *made of* or *made from*.

Seine neue Armbanduhr ist aus Gold.
His new watch is made of gold.

Außer

Außer signifies that someone or something is *excluded* or *excepted*.

Außer seinem Vetter sind alle Verwandten eingeladen worden.
Except for his cousin, all the relatives are invited.

Das Resultat ist leider noch nicht außer Zweifel.
Unfortunately, the result is still in doubt (is not without doubt).

Bei

Bei is used to describe proximity to a point in time; it is sometimes translated as *while* or *during*.

Beim Duschen ist er hingefallen.
He fell down while showering.

Was machen die Wanderer bei schlechtem Wetter?
What do the hikers do during bad weather?

When **bei** describes proximity to an object or a spatial area, it means *at, by,* or *near*.

Der Vater stand mit einem langen Gesicht bei der Tür.
The father stood at the door with a sad face.

Liegt Kleinflottbeck bei Hamburg?
Is Kleinflottbeck near Hamburg?

Gegenüber

Gegenüber means *opposite* or *across from.* This preposition often is placed at the end of the prepositional phrase if the object of the preposition is a pronoun or an animate noun.

> Gegenüber dem Schreibtisch stand eine alte Stehlampe.
> *An old floor lamp stood across from the desk.*

> Wir sitzen ihm gegenüber.
> *We sit opposite him.*

Mit

Mit is most commonly translated as *with* and usually means that someone or something is in the company of someone or something else. Its opposite is **ohne** (*without*).

> Onkel Ludwig ist mit Tante Gerda spazieren gegangen.
> *Uncle Ludwig went strolling with Aunt Gerda.*

Mit also means *with* when it is used to describe the means by which something is done.

> Warum müssen die Lehrlinge mit den Händen arbeiten?
> *Why do the apprentices have to work with their hands?*

Mit is used to describe a mode of travel and is translated as *by.*

> Wir fahren nach Paris mit dem Zug.
> *We're traveling to Paris by train.*

Nach

Nach is often translated as *after* and is the opposite of **vor** (*before*).

> Nach dem Fußballspiel gingen alle ins Café.
> *After the soccer match, everyone went to the cafe.*

It also means *according to*; in this usage, it follows its noun object.

> Meiner Meinung nach ist das reiner Quatsch!
> *In my opinion (according to me), that's pure nonsense!*

> Das muss man dem Gesetz nach tun.
> *You have to do that according to the law.*

In addition, **nach** can mean *to* when signifying movement to a place such as a city or a country. It has a special use in the phrase **nach Hause**, meaning *home* or *homeward.*

> Um wie viel Uhr fährt der Zug nach Venedig?
> *At what time does the train for Venice leave?*

> Ich gehe jetzt nach Hause.
> *I'm going home now.*

Nach Hause has a counterpart with the preposition **zu**: **zu Hause**, which means *at home.*

Seit

Seit means *since* and is used to indicate time from a point in the past up to the present. It is often translated as *for* when used with increments of time (for example, day, month, and year), but as *since* when used with events in time.

> Ich wohne seit acht Jahren in einem Vorort von Stuttgart.
> *I've been living in a suburb of Stuttgart for eight years.*

> Wir haben seit seiner Abreise nichts von ihm gehört.
> *We haven't heard anything from him since his departure.*

Von

Von is the opposite of **nach** and **zu** (*to*) and means *from* when used to describe where someone or something originates.

> Erik ist noch nicht vom Hauptbahnhof zurückgekommen.
> *Erik still hasn't come back from the main railway station.*

> Ich habe diesen Ring von meiner Freundin bekommen.
> *I got this ring from my girlfriend.*

Von is also used to tell who created something; in this usage, it is translated as *by*.

> Das ist ein Roman von Thomas Mann.
> *This is a novel by Thomas Mann.*

Von is used to describe a moment in time and is often used together with **bis** (*until*).

> Klaus wohnte vom 5. Mai bis zum 10. Juni in Bayern.
> *Klaus lived in Bavaria from the fifth of May until the tenth of June.*

In the passive voice, **von** is used to indicate *by whom* some action is performed.

> Die ganze Stadt wurde von den Soldaten zerstört.
> *The whole city was destroyed by the soldiers.*

Zu

Zu is used to tell *to* whom or *to* what place someone is going. When the object is a person, it is often translated as *to _____'s house*.

> Wir fahren jeden Sommer zu Verwandten in Paris.
> *We travel to our relatives' house in Paris every summer.*

> Führt dieser enge Weg zum Stadtpark?
> *Does this narrow path lead to the city park?*

Zu is used in the special expression **zu Hause**, meaning *at home*.

> Ich war den ganzen Tag zu Hause.
> *I was at home all day.*

See **nach Hause** above to compare the two expressions.

Übung   15-3

Fill in each blank with any appropriate noun or noun phrase.

1. Hast du noch nicht von _____ gehört?

2. Thomas wohnt seit _____ in Darmstadt.

3. Die Touristen werden bei _____ übernachten.

4. Haben Sie die interessanten Artikel von _____ gelesen?

5. Der Weg zu _____ ist auf der anderen Seite des Flusses.

6. Ich habe einen Bericht darüber aus _____ geschrieben.

7. Außer _____ wurden alle Soldaten gerettet.

8. Seine Eltern wollen mit _____ sprechen.

9. Was machen wir nach _____?

10. _____ gegenüber sitzt eine fremdartige Frau.

11. Ist Köpenick bei _____?

12. Er arbeitet jetzt mit _____.

13. Sie bleiben vom _____ bis zum vierten Oktober hier.

14. Werdet ihr dorthin mit _____ fahren?

15. In dem Laden hat sie eine alte Uhr aus _____ gefunden.

Accusative-Dative Prepositions

There is a group of German prepositions that can take either the dative or the accusative case. They function very much like a small group of English prepositions.

in   *into*
on   *onto*

The prepositions *in* and *on* are used to show location.

> *They live in New York.*
> *The book was on the table.*

The prepositions *into* and *onto* are used to show movement toward a place.

> *He went into their house.*
> *I threw it onto the table.*

German, using a much larger group of prepositions, differentiates between location and movement by the use of the dative and accusative cases.

an	*at*	über	*over*
auf	*on, onto*	unter	*under*
hinter	*behind*	vor	*in front of, before*
in	*in, into*	zwischen	*between*
neben	*next to*		

These prepositions take two cases, because they are used with two different categories of verbs: (1) verbs that indicate location and (2) verbs that indicate movement from one location to another.

> Ich sitze **im** (**in dem**) Garten.
> *I'm sitting in the garden.* (location)

> Ich laufe **in den** Garten.
> *I run into the garden.* (movement)

Following are some commonly used verbs that show location and movement.

Location		Movement	
arbeiten	*work*	fahren	*drive*
hängen	*hang*	gehen	*go*
liegen	*lie*	legen	*lay*
sitzen	*sit*	stellen	*put, place*
stehen	*stand*	werfen	*throw*

There are many more verbs of this type than those listed. To know which category a verb belongs to, determine if it indicates location or movement. For example, to know the category of the verb **schreiben** (*to write*), ask if it can be done at a location without having to move from one place to another. The answer is yes; therefore, **schreiben** is a location verb. To know the category of the verb **laufen** (*to run*), ask if it can be done at a location without having to move from one place to another. The answer is no; therefore, **laufen** is a movement verb.

Nouns that follow accusative-dative prepositions are in either the dative or the accusative case, and adjectives that modify these nouns have the appropriate adjective endings for those cases.

Masculine nouns

hinter dem alten Mann (*location*)	*behind the old man*
hinter den alten Mann (*movement*)	*behind the old man*
neben einem roten Wagen (*location*)	*next to a red car*
neben einen roten Wagen (*movement*)	*next to a red car*

Feminine nouns

an der breiten Tür (*location*)	*at the wide door*
an die breite Tür (*movement*)	*to the wide door*
vor einer netten Frau (*location*)	*in front of a nice woman*
vor eine nette Frau (*movement*)	*in front of a nice woman*

Neuter nouns

auf dem großen Haus (*location*)	*on the large house*
auf das große Haus (*movement*)	*onto the large house*
unter einem alten Dach (*location*)	*under an old roof*
unter ein altes Dach (*movement*)	*under an old roof*

Plural nouns

in den fremden Ländern (*location*)	*in the foreign lands*
in die fremden Länder (*movement*)	*into the foreign lands*
zwischen meinen Eltern (*location*)	*between my parents*
zwischen meine Eltern (*movement*)	*between my parents*

The accusative declension of feminine and neuter nouns with **der**-words and **ein**-words identifies gender in a prepositional phrase, just as it does when nouns are used as direct objects.

Direct object	Object of accusative-dative preposition
die nette Frau	vor **die** nette Frau
eine nett**e** Frau	vor eine nett**e** Frau
das alte Dach	unter **das** alte Dach
ein alt**es** Dach	unter ein alt**es** Dach

Examples of sentences with accusative-dative prepositions follow.

> Der Stuhl stand an **dem neuen Tisch**.
> *The chair stood by the new table.*

> Ich stellte den Stuhl an **den neuen Tisch**.
> *I placed the chair by the new table.*

> Wir waren letzten Monat auf **einer langen Reise**.
> *We were on a long trip last month.*

> Morgen fahren wir auf **eine lange Reise**.
> *Tomorrow we're going on a long trip.*

> Der Junge verbirgt sich hinter **jenem großen Haus**.
> *The boy hides behind that big house.*

> Der Junge lief hinter **jenes große Haus**.
> *The boy ran behind that big house.*

> Sie hat das Geld in **ihren Taschen**.
> *She has the money in her pockets.*

> Sie steckte das Geld in **ihre Taschen**.
> *She put the money in her pockets.*

When accusative-dative prepositions are used with pronouns that refer to *animate* nouns, the prepositional phrase consists of preposition + accusative/dative pronoun.

> Ich warte **auf ihn**.
> *I'm waiting for him.*

> Wir denken oft **an sie**.
> *We often think of them.*

If you ask the question *whom* with an accusative-dative preposition, the nominative **wer** changes to the dative (**wem**) or the accusative (**wen**), depending on whether the meaning of the preposition shows location or movement.

> Ich will neben Helga sitzen.
> **Neben wem** willst du sitzen?
> *Next to whom do you want to sit?*

> Sie schreibt über den Feind.
> **Über wen** schreibt sie?
> *About whom is she writing?*

Sometimes *location* is not the meaning desired with these prepositions. For example, **warten auf** requires the accusative case, because the meaning is not *waiting **on top of** someone* but rather *waiting **for** someone*. There are numerous instances where the concept of *location* would seem strange or out of place. In these instances, it is usual to use the accusative case in place of the dative, even though the idea of *movement* is not apparent in the meaning of the verb-and-preposition combination. Some examples follow.

denken an (*accusative*)	*to think about*
sich freuen auf (*accusative*)	*to look forward to*
sich freuen über (*accusative*)	*to be glad about*
schreiben über (*accusative*)	*to write about*
sich verlieben in (*accusative*)	*to fall in love with*

It is wise to consult a dictionary when in doubt about the proper use of cases after an accusative-dative preposition.

Übung   16-1

Rewrite each sentence, using the appropriate form of the word or phrase in parentheses to fill in the blank.

1. Eine Fledermaus ist zwischen _____ geflogen.

    a. (die Häuser)   _____

    b. (die Kirche und die Schule)   _____

    c. (ein Turm und ein Haus)   _____

2. Wer sitzt neben _____?

    a. (dein Bruder)   _____

    b. (er)   _____

    c. (Ihre Tante)   _____

    d. (die kleinen Fenster)   _____

3. Der bellende Hund läuft an _____.

    a. (die Tür)   _____

    b. (das offene Fenster)   _____

    c. (der große Spiegel)   _____

4. Kleiner Benno versteckte sich hinter _____.

    a. (ein großer Baum)   _____

    b. (der Schrank)   _____

    c. (die blauen Gardinen)   _____

    d. (eine Mauer)   _____

Übung	16-2

Fill in each blank with the appropriate preposition. Choose from **auf**, **hinter**, **in**, *and* **unter**.

1. Herr Schäfer wohnt jetzt _____ einem Vorort von Berlin.

2. Warum sitzt der Mann oben _____ dem Dach?

3. Der alte Hund ist _____ dem großen Tisch eingeschlafen.

4. Wie lange musstest du _____ ihn warten?

5. Das Leben _____ dem Lande ist so entspannend.

6. Wir waren _____ den Zuschauern im Theater.

7. Ich bin _____ zehn Minuten wieder da.

8. Gudrun hat seinen Mantel _____ den Schrank gehängt.

9. Karin versteckt sich _____ der Tür und wartet auf ihren Bruder.

10. Liegen meine Sachen _____ dem Tisch?

Multiple Usages

The meaning of the accusative-dative prepositions shown in the lists and examples above is their *basic meaning*. Accusative-dative prepositions, however, have more than one use and therefore have to be translated into English appropriately to achieve the intended meaning.

An

An is used to show location at or movement toward a vertical object or surface (for example, a door, wall, or window).

> Das Porträt hängt an der Wand.
> *The portrait is hanging on the wall.*

> Ich habe das Porträt an die Wand gehängt.
> *I hung the portrait on the wall.*

An is used with days, as well as the time of day.

> Ich komme entweder am Morgen oder am Freitag.
> *I'll come either in the morning or on Friday.*

> An solchen Tagen muss man vorsichtig sein.
> *One has to be careful on such days.*

It is also used to signify an approximation.

> Es waren an die hundert Besucher in dem kleinen Saal.
> *There were about a hundred visitors in the little hall.*

Auf

Auf is used to show location at or movement on or onto a horizontal object or surface.

> Warum liegen meine Hemden auf dem Boden?
> *Why are my shirts on the floor?*

> Jemand hat meine Hemden auf den Boden geworfen.
> *Someone threw my shirts on the floor.*

Auf is also used in certain set expressions.

auf dem Lande	*in the country*
auf der Post	*at the post office*
Auf deutsch, bitte!	*In German, please.*
auf Urlaub	*on vacation/furlough*
Auf Wiedersehen!	*Good-bye.*

Hinter

Hinter means *behind* or *in back of* and is the opposite of **vor** (*before, in front of*).

> Hinter unserem Garten liegt ein alter Friedhof.
> *There's an old cemetery behind our garden.*

> Sie stellt das Buch hinter die Gardine.
> *She puts the book behind the curtains.*

In

In means *in* or *into* and is used to indicate location within something or movement into something.

> Der arme Mann hat jetzt 50 Euro in seiner Hand.
> *The poor man now has 50 euros in his hand.*

> Bitte hängen Sie Ihre Jacke in den Schrank.
> *Please hang up your jacket in the wardrobe.*

In is also used to describe actions in certain timeframes.

> In zwei Jahren werde ich damit fertig sein.
> *I'll be through with it in two years.*

It is also used to describe an abstract state or a state of mind.

> Ich bin in Gedanken.
> *I'm deep in thought.*

> Sie war in Sorge.
> *She was worried.*

> Sie sind in tiefer Trauer.
> *They are in deep mourning.*

> Die Kinder waren in Unruhe.
> *The children were upset.*

Neben

Neben is used to indicate location or movement next to a person or thing. It can mean *next to* or *beside.*

> Der Taschendieb stellte sich neben mich und wartete.
> *The pickpocket came up next to me and waited.*

> Ist die Kirche neben dem Rathaus?
> *Is the church next to city hall?*

Über

Über signifies that someone or something is higher than someone or something else. It is the opposite of **unter** (*under*).

> Eine Laterne hing über dem kleinen Tisch.
> *A lantern hung over the little table.*

> Wilde Enten fliegen über den blauen See hinüber.
> *Wild ducks fly over/across the blue lake.*

Über is also used to indicate that an amount of something is greater than a stated level.

> Der alte Graf ist über neunzig.
> *The old count is more than ninety.*

Über is used to express the lapse of a certain amount of time.

> Es ist drei Stunden über die Zeit.
> *It's three hours past the time.*

Unter

Unter is the opposite of **über** and signifies that someone or something is lower than someone or something else.

> Die wichtigen Dokumente sind unter einem Buch versteckt.
> *The important documents are hidden under a book.*

> Der Düsenjäger ist unter eine dunkle Wolke hinuntergeflogen.
> *The jet fighter flew under a dark cloud.*

It is also used to indicate that an amount of something is less than a stated level.

> Der junge Mann lügt. Er ist noch unter achtzehn Jahren.
> *The young man is lying. He's less than eighteen years old.*

When used with groups of people or things, **unter** means *among.*

> Unter den billigen Ringen sah er nur einen goldenen Ring.
> *Among the inexpensive rings he saw only one gold ring.*

> Herr Bauer ist unter den Lehrern der Populärste.
> *Mr. Bauer is the most popular among the teachers.*

Vor

Vor signifies that someone or something is on the visible side of someone or something else. It is the opposite of **hinter** (*behind*).

Vor der Stadtmauer standen zwei Ritter.
Two knights stood in front of the city wall.

Er legte die Zeitungen vor die Tür.
He laid the newspapers in front of the door.

With expressions of time, **vor** is translated as *ago*.

vor zehn Tagen   *ten days ago*
vor einem Jahr   *a year ago*

When telling time, **vor** means *before, of,* or *to*.

Es ist Viertel vor zwei.
It's a quarter to two / before two / of two.

Zwischen

Zwischen means to be *between* two or more persons or things and can be used to show location or movement.

Der neue Schreibtisch steht zwischen dem Sessel und dem Sofa.
The new desk is between the armchair and the sofa.

Die neue Schülerin setzte sich zwischen zwei schüchterne Jungen.
The new pupil sat down between two shy boys.

Übung	16-3

Fill in each blank with any appropriate word or phrase.

1. Ich habe oft an _____ gedacht.

2. Zwei Stühle standen an _____.

3. Eine große Wiese liegt hinter _____.

4. Du sollst das Geld in _____ stecken.

5. Wer steigt auf _____?

6. Anna Schneider ist Professorin an _____ geworden.

7. Sagen Sie das bitte auf _____.

8. Ein Bild eines alten Herrn hängt über _____.

9. Deine Bücher liegen zwischen _____.

10. Vor _____ stand ein großer, alter Tannenbaum.

11. Der älteste Kandidat ist unter _____ .

12. Das neue Restaurant ist neben _____ .

13. Ich habe mich in _____ verliebt.

14. Ein toter Sperling liegt auf _____ .

15. Sie haben sich über _____ sehr gefreut.

Übung   16-4

Circle the preposition that best completes each sentence.

1. Bitte hängen Sie Ihre Sachen _____ den Schrank.   an | auf | in

2. Mein Vater denkt oft _____ meine Mutter.   vor | neben | an

3. Jemand stand _____ dem Tor.   hinter | zwischen | aus

4. Benno lief _____ die Tür und wartete auf seinen Vater.   an | ins | unter

5. Wer sitzt _____ dem Dach?   bis | wider | auf

6. Freust du dich schon _____ die Ferien?   vor | auf | hinter

7. Sie will das Bild _____ das Bett hängen.   im | über | zwischen

8. Er war _____ zwei Wochen in der Hauptstadt.   von | neben | vor

9. Habt ihr lange _____ mich gewartet?   auf | an | für

10. Niemand steht _____ Karl und Heidi.   in | zu | zwischen

Genitive Prepositions

The genitive prepositions require nouns in a prepositional phrase to be in the genitive case. A list of common genitive prepositions follows.

diesseits	*this side of*	trotz	*in spite of, despite*
jenseits	*that side of*	außerhalb	*outside of*
anstatt, statt	*instead of*	innerhalb	*inside of*
während	*during*	oberhalb	*above*
wegen	*because of*	unterhalb	*beneath*

Notice how many of the genitive prepositions have *of* in their meaning. The English concept of possession using the word *of* appears in German as the genitive case.

die Farbe **des Wagens**	*the color **of the car***
wegen **des Wagens**	*because **of the car***

Note: **Trotz** is also often used with the dative case.

trotz allem	*in spite of everything*
trotz dem drohenden Krieg	*in spite of the impending war*

Wegen can precede or follow its prepositional object.

wegen einer Krankheit	*because of an illness*
seiner Kinder wegen	*because of his children*

Examples of sentences with genitive prepositional phrases follow, showing a variety of noun objects.

Wir wohnen diesseits **der holländischen Grenze**.
We live on this side of the Dutch border.

Frankreich ist jenseits **des Flusses**.
France is on the other side of the river.

Anstatt **eines goldenen Ringes** befand sich in der Schublade ein Nagel.
Instead of a gold ring, there was a nail in the drawer.

Während **eines Gewitters** bleiben wir zu Hause.
During a rainstorm we stay at home.

Erhardt ist wegen **seiner Eltern** in Sorge.
Erhardt is worried because of his parents.

Trotz **ihrer Krankheit** kam Helga zur Arbeit.
In spite of her illness, Helga came to work.

Sie haben die letzten drei Jahre außerhalb **der Vereinigten Staaten** verbracht.
They have spent the last three years outside of the United States.

Innerhalb **des kleinen Dorfes** sind noch viele alte Häuser zu finden.
You can still find a lot of old houses inside the little village.

Oberhalb **der Schule** führt ein Weg auf den Berg hinauf.
Above the school a path leads up the mountain.

Unterhalb **eines breiten Baumes** befindet sich eine Bank.
There's a bench beneath a broad tree.

The adjective ending in the genitive case for all genders and the plural is **-en**.

des gut**en** Mannes
der gut**en** Frau
des gut**en** Kindes
der gut**en** Menschen

Übung 17-1

Rewrite each sentence, using the appropriate form of the word or phrase in parentheses to fill in the blank.

1. Ich kann wegen _____ leider nicht kommen.

   a. (das Gewitter) _____

   b. (eine Erkältung) _____

   c. (sein Tod) _____

2. Während _____ waren wir am Bodensee.

   a. (die Ferien) _____

   b. (unser Urlaub) _____

   c. (die wärmsten Tage) _____

3. Eine enge Straße führte oberhalb _____.

   a. (das kleine Rathaus) _____

   b. (ein schöner Park) _____

   c. (die Gaststätte) _____

4. Trotz _____ geht mein Großvater täglich zur Arbeit.

    a. (das Wetter)   _____

    b. (sein hohes Alter)   _____

    c. (die furchtbare Kälte)   _____

5. Statt _____ ist ein junger Arzt gekommen.

    a. (ein Pfarrer)   _____

    b. (seine Verwandten)   _____

    c. (eine Krankenschwester)   _____

Two German words that look like prepositions use the prefix **wes-**: **weshalb** and **weswegen**. Both can function as an interrogative and a conjunction and have a variety of meanings: as interrogatives, *why* and *for what reason*, and as conjunctions, *on account of which* and *therefore*. They do not require the use of the genitive case, because they are not prepositions; they behave like other interrogatives and conjunctions. These two words share the same meanings and usage and are synonyms of **warum**.

> Weshalb bist du in schlechter Laune?
> *Why are you in a bad mood?*

> Er sah mich nicht, weswegen er nach Hause ging.
> *He didn't see me; therefore he went home.*

Pronouns cannot occur in genitive prepositional phrases. Instead, they take on a new form (but with only certain of the prepositions) and are considered adverbs.

With the suffix **-halben**

ich	meinethalben	*for my sake, on my behalf*
du	deinethalben	*for your sake, on your behalf*
er	seinethalben	*for his (its) sake, on his (its) behalf*
sie (*sing.*)	ihrethalben	*for her (its) sake, on her (its) behalf*
es	seinethalben	*for its sake, on its behalf*
wir	unserthalben	*for our sake, on our behalf*
ihr	eurethalben	*for your sake, on your behalf*
sie (*pl.*)	ihrethalben	*for their sake, on their behalf*

With the suffix **-seits**

ich	meinerseits	*as far as I am concerned*
du	deinerseits	*as far as you are concerned*
er	seinerseits	*as far as he (it) is concerned*
sie (*sing.*)	ihrerseits	*as far as she (it) is concerned*
es	seinerseits	*as far as it is concerned*
wir	unserseits	*as far as we are concerned*
ihr	eurerseits	*as far as you are concerned*
sie (*pl.*)	ihrerseits	*as far as they are concerned*

With the suffix -wegen

ich	meinetwegen	*because of me, for my part*
du	deinetwegen	*because of you, for your part*
er	seinetwegen	*because of him (it), for his (its) part*
sie (*sing.*)	ihretwegen	*because of her (it), for her (its) part*
es	seinetwegen	*because of it, for its part*
wir	unsertwegen	*because of us, for our part*
ihr	euretwegen	*because of you, for your part*
sie (*pl.*)	ihretwegen	*because of them, for their part*

Übung 17-2

Fill in the blank with the appropriate preposition. Choose from **während**, **anstatt**, **wegen**, *and* **diesseits**.

1. Wohnen Sie jetzt _____ der Alpen?

2. _____ eines Briefes schickte ich dir eine Postkarte.

3. _____ des Sommers sind wir oft am See.

4. Die Kinder müssen _____ des Schnees zu Hause bleiben.

5. _____ eines Geschenks habe ich eine Rechnung bekommen.

6. _____ des Frühlings arbeiten wir auf einem Bauernhof.

7. _____ des Mittelmeers ist das Klima viel besser.

8. Klaus hat seines Fehlens _____ viele Vorlesungen versäumt.

9. Wo haben Sie _____ des Krieges gedient?

10. _____ einer Armbanduhr hat sie ihm einen Wecker geschenkt.

Übung 17-3

Fill in each blank with any appropriate word or phrase.

1. Innerhalb _____ ist die Sicherheit gegen den Feind besser.

2. Unterhalb _____ befindet sich ein schöner Bach.

3. Trotz _____ ist der Mann wirklich nur 40 Jahre alt.

4. Der Autobahnverkehr ist wieder wegen _____ gestört.

5. Sie haben ein Sommerhaus diesseits _____ .

6. Ich verbrachte drei Wochen während _____ in Berlin.

7. Oberhalb _____ waren große Weinberge.

8. Jenseits _____ liegt Afrika.

9. Außerhalb _____ befinden sich schöne Aussichtspunkte.

10. Statt _____ brachte sie ihm Apfelsaft.

11. Innerhalb _____ fühlt man sich sicher und zufrieden.

12. Trotz _____ bestand sie die schwere Prüfung.

13. Während _____ hatten wir viel Regen und Nebel.

14. Wegen _____ mussten wir in einem Lokal feiern.

15. Statt _____ hat mein Vater einen gebrauchten Wagen gekauft.

Prepositional Adverbs

English treats inanimate and animate noun and pronoun objects of a preposition in the same way. Prepositional phrases are structured as preposition + object.

with a friend   *with him*
near the store   *near it*

German has an identical structure with regard to animate nouns and pronouns. Prepositional phrases are structured as preposition + noun or pronoun.

mit einem Freund	*with a friend*
mit ihm	*with him*
neben meiner Lehrerin	*next to my teacher*
neben ihr	*next to her*

When the object of a preposition is an inanimate noun, the same structure of a prepositional phrase applies. But when the inanimate noun is replaced by a pronoun, the structure changes: The prepositional phrase becomes a *prepositional adverb* (often called a *pronominal adverb*), which is structured as **da-** + preposition.

mit dem Wagen	*by car*
damit	*by it, with it*
neben dem Laden	*next to the store*
daneben	*next to it*

If the preposition begins with a vowel, **-r-** is added to **da-**.

in dem Haus	*in the house*
darin	*in it*
auf dem Dach	*on the roof*
darauf	*on it*

Sometimes **hier-** can be used as the prefix instead of **da-**, particularly when the *nearness* of something is being stressed. The prepositional adverb structured with **da-**, however, is usually preferable.

hierauf
hierbei
hierdurch
hiermit

Interrogatives

If you ask the question *whom* with a preposition, the appropriate form of **wer** (dative **wem** or accusative **wen**) is used.

Mit wem spricht er?
Whom is he talking with?

Auf wen warten Sie?
Whom are you waiting for?

But if you ask *what* with a preposition, **was** is not combined with the preposition to form a prepositional phrase. Instead, a prepositional adverb is used with the structure **wo-** + preposition.

vor der Tür	*in front of the door*
wovor?	*in front of what?*
mit dem Zug	*by train*
womit?	*by what?, with what?*

If the preposition begins with a vowel, **-r-** is added to **wo-**.

in dem Haus	*in the house*
worin?	*in what?*
auf dem Dach	*on the roof*
worauf?	*on what?*

The following example sentences illustrate prepositional adverbs formed with **da(r)-**.

Er spricht **über die Krise**.
He's speaking about the crisis.
Er spricht **darüber**.
He's speaking about it.

Ich bin **gegen den Krieg**.
I'm against the war.
Ich bin **dagegen**.
I'm against it.

Sie bittet **um meine Adresse**.
She asks for my address.
Sie bittet **darum**.
She asks for it.

Niemand spricht **von dem Problem**.
No one talks about the problem.
Niemand spricht **davon**.
No one talks about it.

Er fragt **nach meiner Gesundheit**.
He asks about my health.
Er fragt **danach**.
He asks about it.

The following example sentences illustrate prepositional adverbs formed with **wo(r)-**.

Er träumt **von seinen Ferien**.
He dreams of his vacation.
Wovon träumt er?
What's he dreaming about?

Er fährt **mit der Bahn** in die Stadt.
He goes by train to the city.
Womit fährt er in die Stadt?
What (transport) does he take to the city?

Er spricht **über seine Jugend**.
He speaks about his youth.
Worüber spricht er?
What's he speaking about?

Sie sind **gegen den Krieg**.
They are against the war.
Wogegen sind sie?
What are they against?

Er bittet **um ein Glas Wein**.
He is asking for a glass of wine.
Worum bittet er?   OR   **Um was** bittet er?
What is he asking for?

Note: Although it breaks the rule that inanimate pronouns form prepositional adverbs, there is a tendency to use **um was** in place of **worum**.

Not all German prepositions can form a prepositional adverb. Those that are used in time expressions, for example, form a question with **wann: bis wann** (*till when*) and **seit wann** (*since when*). But a large number of prepositions *can* form a prepositional adverb with either prefix treated above, **da(r)-** or **wo(r)-**. Following is a list of commonly used prepositions and their forms as prepositional adverbs.

Preposition	**da(r)-** form	**wo(r)-** form
an	daran	woran
auf	darauf	worauf
aus	daraus	woraus
bei	dabei	wobei
durch	dadurch	wodurch
für	dafür	wofür
gegen	dagegen	wogegen
in	darin	worin
mit	damit	womit
nach	danach	wonach
neben	daneben	woneben
über	darüber	worüber
um	darum	worum
unter	darunter	worunter
von	davon	wovon
vor	davor	wovor
zu	dazu	wozu

Some prepositions take an accusative object, and others take a dative object. Still others can take objects of either of these cases. However, when one of these prepositions becomes part of a prepositional adverb, case no longer matters: You cannot distinguish the accusative from the dative.

Accusative case	für deine Idee	*for your idea*
Prepositional adverbs	dafür	wofür
Accusative case	in den Garten	*into the garden*
Prepositional adverbs	darin	worin
Dative case	mit der Straßenbahn	*by streetcar*
Prepositional adverbs	damit	womit
Dative case	an dem Fenster	*at the window*
Prepositional adverbs	daran	woran

The same sentence with different prepositional objects requires distinguishing between animate and inanimate objects when changing the prepositional objects from a noun to a pronoun.

Animate object
_____

Erich hat auf seinen Bruder gewartet.
Erich waited for his brother.
Erich hat **auf ihn** gewartet.
Erich waited for him.

Inanimate object
_____

Erich hat auf den Zug gewartet.
Erich waited for the train.
Erich hat **darauf** gewartet.
Erich waited for it.

The question formed with these prepositional objects differs as well.

Auf wen hat Erich gewartet?
Whom did Erich wait for?

Worauf hat Erich gewartet?
What did Erich wait for?

Übung   18-1

*Form prepositional adverbs with **da(r)-** and **wo(r)-** for each of the prepositions in parentheses.*

EXAMPLE   (von)   _____davon_____   _____wovon_____

1. (vor)   _____   _____

2. (bei)   _____   _____

3. (in)   _____   _____

4. (auf)   _____   _____

5. (mit)   _____   _____

6. (zu)   _____   _____

7. (an)   _____   _____

8. (aus)   _____   _____

9. (neben)   _____   _____

10. (durch)   _____   _____

11. (nach)   _____   _____

12. (für)   _____   _____

13. (gegen)   _____   _____

14. (um)   _____   _____

15. (über)   _____   _____

Übung	18-2

Rewrite each sentence, changing the prepositional phrase in boldface to a prepositional adverb with **da(r)-**.

1. Haben Sie mehr als 200 Euro **für den Anzug** gezahlt?

   _____

2. Ich habe mich sehr **über seinen Brief** gefreut.

   _____

3. Man muss **gegen falsche Meinungen** kämpfen.

   _____

4. Der Graf herrschte **über ein großes Land**.

   _____

5. Er fürchtet sich **vor den Gefahren des Lebens**.

   _____

6. Gudrun denkt oft **an ihren Aufenthalt in Madrid**.

   _____

7. Was wollen Sie **mit dem Schießgewehr**?

   _____

8. Erich hat noch nichts **von dem großen Autorennen** gehört.

_____

9. Herr Schneider hat **für die Zukunft seiner Familie** gesorgt.

_____

10. Mein älterer Bruder hat mir **mit allem** geholfen.

_____

A prepositional adverb formed with **da(r)-** can be used to introduce another clause. The translation of such a prepositional adverb is often the meaning of the preposition plus the words _the fact_ or _the aspect_, but not always.

> Er denkt daran, dass er jetzt endlich in Amerika ist.
> _He thinks about the fact that he's now finally in America._

> Erinnerst du dich daran, wann du den Wagen kauftest?
> _Do you remember when you bought the car?_

> Ich freue mich darauf euch wieder besuchen zu dürfen.
> _I'm looking forward to being able to visit you again._

> Sie interessiert sich dafür wie man Hochhäuser baut.
> _She's interested in how you build tall buildings._

When the relative pronoun _what_ combines with a preposition, a prepositional adverb formed with **wo(r)-** is used.

> Ich frage mich woran Helga jetzt denkt.
> _I wonder what Helga is thinking about now._

> Das ist alles, woran er sich erinnern kann.
> _That's all that he can remember._

Übung   18-3

Rewrite each sentence as a question, changing the prepositional phrase in boldface to a prepositional adverb with **wo(r)-**.

1. Sie interessieren sich **für die Chemie**.

_____

2. Die armen Bürger riefen **nach besseren Zeiten**.

_____

3. Ich habe oft **an die Vergangenheit** gedacht.

_____

4. Die Eltern hoffen **auf eine bessere Zukunft für ihre Kinder**.

_____

5. Ein kleiner Knabe spielt **mit einem scharfen Messer**.

_____

6. Seine Eifersucht ist ein Beweis **für seine Liebe**.

_____

7. Ich freute mich sehr **auf das Wiedersehen mit meinem Onkel**.

_____

8. Der Arzt fragte **nach ihrer Gesundheit**.

_____

9. Die neugierige Katze lief **an das Fenster**.

_____

10. Er fürchtet sich **vor allem, was er nicht versteht**.

_____

Übung   18-4

Rewrite each sentence, changing the prepositional adverb in boldface to any appropriate prepositional phrase.

1. Ich habe mich sehr **darauf** gefreut.

_____

2. Was macht ihr **damit**?

_____

3. Sie denkt wieder **daran**.

_____

4. Karl wird **danach** fragen.

_____

5. Interessierst du dich **dafür**?

_____

Write an answer to each question, changing the prepositional adverb in boldface to any appropriate prepositional phrase.

6. **Worauf** warten Sie?

   _____

7. **Worüber** freuen Sie sich?

   _____

8. **Woran** hat er sich erinnert?

   _____

9. **Wogegen** schützen sie sich?

   _____

10. **Wofür** sorgen die Eltern?

   _____

Verbs with a Prepositional Object

Many English verbs can only be used with certain prepositions. Even though a sentence may be understood if a wrong preposition is used, the correct preposition is important in conveying the proper meaning of the sentence. The following sentence uses the correct preposition.

> *I wait for Mary.*

You cannot say *I wait **to** Mary* or *I wait **at** Mary*. Only the preposition *for* is appropriate for the verb *wait*.

German is no different. Certain German verbs require the use of a specific preposition with a pronoun or noun phrase that follows. Those two elements—the preposition and the phrase that follows—are called the *prepositional object*.

Whether a verb is regular or irregular or whether it requires **haben** or **sein** in the perfect tenses has no bearing on the choice of prepositions. Following is a list of commonly used verbs, along with the preposition(s) that each requires. (The case required with accusative-dative prepositions is identified by (*acc.*) or (*dat.*).)

abhängen von	Es hängt **von** deiner Gesundheit ab. *It depends on your health.*
antworten auf (*acc.*)	Er antwortete dem Dozenten **auf** die Frage. *He answered the lecturer's question.*
arbeiten an (*dat.*)	Arbeiten Sie noch **an** Ihrer Dissertation? *Are you still working on your dissertation?*
aufhören mit	Hören Sie da**mit** auf! *Stop that!*
aufpassen auf (*acc.*)	Ich passe **auf** die Kinder auf. *I look after the children.*
sich bedanken bei	Ich möchte mich **bei** Ihnen bedanken. *I'd like to thank you.*

sich beklagen bei	Sie hat sich **bei** ihrem Rechtsanwalt beklagt. *She complained to her attorney.*
sich beklagen über (*acc.*)	Martin beklagte sich **über** die kalte Suppe. *Martin complained about the cold soup.*
bekommen von	**Von** wem hast du es bekommen? *From whom did you get it?*
sich beschäftigen mit	Er beschäftigt sich **mit** dem neuen Computer. *He's busy with the new computer.*
sich bewerben um (*acc.*)	Der Reisende hat sich **um** ein Visum beworben. *The traveler applied for a visa.*
bezahlen für	Haben Sie **für** das Essen bezahlt? *Did you pay for the meal?*
bitten um (*acc.*)	Darf ich **um** Ihren Namen bitten? *May I ask your name?*
blicken auf (*acc.*)	Die Touristen blicken **auf** den schönen See. *The tourists look at the beautiful lake.*
denken an (*acc.*)	Ich denke oft **an** Oma. *I often think about Grandma.*
erzählen von	Frau Kamps hat **von** ihrer Spanienreise erzählt. *Mrs. Kamps told about her trip to Spain.*
fahren mit (*transport*)	Ich fahre lieber **mit** dem Zug / mit dem Bus / mit der Straßenbahn. *I prefer to travel by train / bus / streetcar.*
fragen nach	Hat jemand **nach** uns gefragt? *Has anyone asked about us?*
sich freuen auf (*acc.*)	Die Schüler freuen sich schon **auf** die Ferien. *The pupils are already looking forward to vacation.*
sich freuen über (*acc.*)	Ich habe mich **über** deinen letzten Brief gefreut. *I was pleased with your last letter.*
sich fürchten vor (*dat.*)	Der Hund fürchtet sich **vor** den Menschen. *The dog is afraid of people.*
gehen um (*acc.*)	Wie immer ging es **um** das Geld. *As usual, it was a matter of money.*
gehören zu	Angelika gehört **zu** einem Sportverein. *Angelika belongs to a sports club.*
glauben an (*acc.*)	Glaubst du **an** Gott? *Do you believe in God?*
hängen an (*acc.*)	Ich hänge das Bild **an** die Wand. *I hang the picture on the wall.*
hängen an (*dat.*)	Das Bild hängt **an** der Wand. *The picture is hanging on the wall.*

hängen über (*acc.*)	Wer hängte dieses Bild **über** das Bett? *Who hung this picture over the bed?*
hängen über (*dat.*)	Das Bild hängt **über** dem Bett. *The picture is hanging over the bed.*
sich interessieren für	Mein Sohn interessiert sich **für** alle Wissenschaften. *My son is interested in all the sciences.*
kämpfen gegen	Die Soldaten kämpfen **gegen** den Feind. *The soldiers are fighting against the enemy.*
kommen aus	Mein Onkel kommt **aus** Hannover. *My uncle comes from Hanover.*
riechen nach	Hier riecht es **nach** Fisch. *It smells of fish here.*
sein aus (*from*)	Sind Ihre Eltern **aus** Italien? *Are your parents from Italy?*
sein aus (*made of*)	Seine neue Armbanduhr ist **aus** Gold. *His new wristwatch is made of gold.*
sprechen über (*acc.*)	Ich möchte heute **über** ein neues Problem sprechen. *I'd like to speak about a new problem today.*
sprechen von	Wir werden noch da**von** sprechen müssen. *We're still going to have to talk about that.*
suchen nach	Die Katze sucht in allen Ecken **nach** der Maus. *The cat is looking for the mouse in every corner.*
teilnehmen an (*dat.*)	Wir nehmen **an** der Wahl teil. *We take part in the election.*
sich verlassen auf (*acc.*)	Ich kann mich **auf** meinen Bruder verlassen. *I can rely on my brother.*
warnen vor (*dat.*)	Er warnte mich **vor** dem Taschendieb. *He warned me about the pickpocket.*
warten auf (*acc.*)	Wir haben lange **auf** dich gewartet. *We waited a long time for you.*
wohnen bei	Frau Krebs wird **bei** ihrer Schwester wohnen. *Mrs. Krebs is going to live at her sister's house.*

It is important to remember which preposition is required by a verb, because the wrong preposition can convey the wrong meaning. The following sentences both use the verb **sich freuen**.

> Ich freue mich **auf** das Wochenende.
> *I'm looking forward to the weekend.*

> Ich freue mich **über** ihren Brief.
> *I'm happy about her letter.*

As similar as these two sentences are, the verbs convey different meanings—meanings that are derived in part from the prepositions.

There are many such combinations of verbs and prepositions. When adding a new verb to your German vocabulary, it is wise to identify the preposition(s) required (and the case required, if the preposition is an accusative-dative preposition).

Übung	19-1

Fill in the first blank with the missing preposition. In the second blank, write the English translation of the verb-preposition combination.

EXAMPLE   warten __*auf*__   __*to wait for*__

1. teilnehmen _____   _____

2. bitten _____   _____

3. fragen _____   _____

4. wohnen _____   _____

5. sich fürchten _____   _____

6. aufpassen _____   _____

7. sich bewerben _____   _____

8. abhängen _____   _____

9. aufhören _____   _____

10. sprechen _____   _____

11. sich bedanken _____   _____

12. sein _____   _____

13. kommen _____   _____

14. glauben _____   _____

15. kämpfen _____   _____

Übung 19-2

Rewrite each sentence, completing it with the correct form of the phrase in parentheses.

1. Du sollst die Touristen vor _____ warnen.

   a. (diese Gefahr) _____

   b. (die Untersuchungen) _____

   c. (der Taschendieb) _____

2. Ich kann mich immer auf _____ verlassen.

   a. (mein Vater) _____

   b. (die junge Ärztin) _____

   c. (seine Vernunft) _____

3. Wenn er einsam ist, denkt er an _____.

   a. (seine Heimat) _____

   b. (ein guter Freund in Berlin) _____

   c. (sie [*sing.*]) _____

4. Erzählen Sie bitte von _____!

   a. (Ihre Vergangenheit) _____

   b. (das Leben in Amerika) _____

   c. (Ihre Reisen) _____

Übung 19-3

Complete each sentence, filling in the blank with any appropriate word or phrase.

1. Ich möchte mich bei _____ bedanken.

2. Mein Vetter kommt aus _____.

3. Sie kann auf _____ nicht antworten.

4. Interessierst du dich für _____?

5. Ingrid hat die Blumen von _____ bekommen.

6. Es geht wieder um _____.

7. Wer hat für _____ bezahlt?

8. Mein Vater gehört jetzt zu _____.

9. Der Polizist bat mich um _____.

10. Wir fahren lieber mit _____.

Übung	**19-4**

Circle the preposition that best completes each sentence.

1. Viele Leute haben _____ der Wahl teilgenommen.   auf | an | aus

2. Du kannst dich _____ mich verlassen.   auf | für | bei

3. Herr Bauer wohnt wieder _____ seiner Schwester.   vor | auf | bei

4. Die Kinder beschäftigen sich _____ dem Computer.   zu | durch | mit

5. Was hängt _____ dem Tisch?   über | bis | seit

6. Der neue Student kommt _____ Berlin.   auf | vor | aus

7. Ich interessiere mich _____ klassische Musik.   für | nach | gegen

8. Hier riecht es _____ Wein.   vor | auf | nach

9. Wir glauben _____ die Demokratie.   an | aus | von

10. Sie sind _____ einem Bus gefahren.   mit | auf | neben

Adjectives with a Prepositional Object

As with many verbs, certain adjectives require the use of a specific preposition with a pronoun or noun phrase that follows. English and German approach this concept in the same way.

In English, the preposition *for* is commonly used with the adjective *ready*.

> *Are you ready for work?*
> *The doctor is ready for you now.*

This adjective and preposition cannot be translated into German with the ordinary German word for each, **bereit** and **für**. The German adjective **bereit** requires **zu** to form its prepositional object.

It is, therefore, essential to learn a German adjective with the preposition it requires. Some high-frequency adjectives are listed below with the prepositions they require. (The case required with accusative-dative prepositions is identified by (*acc.*) or (*dat.*).)

abhängig von	Das Resultat ist abhängig **von** unseren Bemühungen. *The result is dependent on our efforts.*
arm an (*dat.*)	Das kleine Land ist arm **an** Kohle und Eisen. *The little country is poor in coal and iron.*
aufmerksam auf (*acc.*)	Man muss **auf** die kleinen Kinder aufmerksam sein. *You have to be attentive to the little children.*
bekannt mit	Sind Sie **mit** Herrn Schneider bekannt? *Are you acquainted with Mr. Schneider?*
böse auf (*acc.*)	Meine Mutter war sehr böse **auf** mich. *My mother was very angry with me.*
dankbar für	Wir waren sehr dankbar **für** Ihre Hilfe. *We were very grateful for your help.*

fähig zu	Seid ihr zur Vorbereitung **zu** dem Staatsexamen fähig? *Are you capable of preparing for the graduation exam?*
fertig mit	Sie ist da**mit** fertig. *She's finished with that.*
fertig zu	Er fragt, ob sie **zur** Abreise fertig sind. *He asks if they're ready for departure.*
freundlich zu	Der Chef ist freundlich **zu** der Stenographistin. *The boss is kind to the secretary.*
froh über (*acc.*)	Der älteste Sohn ist froh **über** den neuen Wagen. *The oldest son is happy about the new car.*
gewöhnt an (*acc.*)	Ich bin leider nicht dar**an** gewöhnt. *Unfortunately, I'm not accustomed to that.*
glücklich über (*acc.*)	Waren Sie glücklich **über** die Reise? *Were you happy about the trip?*
neidisch auf (*acc.*)	Warum bin ich so neidisch **auf** sie? *Why am I so jealous of her?*
reich an (*dat.*)	Russland ist noch reich **an** Öl. *Russia is still rich in oil.*
stolz auf (*acc.*)	Die Eltern sind sehr stolz **auf** ihren Sohn. *The parents are very proud of their son.*
überzeugt von	Wir sind noch nicht da**von** überzeugt. *We're still not convinced of it.*
verliebt in (*acc.*)	Sie war **in** den Kronprinzen verliebt. *She was in love with the crown prince.*
verschieden von	Karl ist sehr verschieden **von** seinem Bruder. *Karl is very different from his brother.*
zufrieden mit	Die Kritiker waren zufrieden **mit** der Kunstausstellung. *The critics were satisfied with the art exhibit.*

It is important to remember which preposition is required with an adjective, because the wrong preposition can convey the wrong meaning.

German has many combinations of adjectives and prepositions like those listed above. When adding a new adjective to your German vocabulary, it is wise to identify the preposition(s) required (and the case required, if the preposition is an accusative-dative preposition).

Übung	20-1

Fill in the first blank with the missing preposition. In the second blank, write the English translation of the adjective-preposition combination.

EXAMPLE fertig _mit_   _finished with_

1. verliebt _____   _____

2. bereit _____   _____

3. arm _____   _____

4. reich _____   _____

5. zufrieden _____   _____

6. freundlich _____   _____

7. aufmerksam _____   _____

8. bekannt _____   _____

9. verschieden _____   _____

10. böse _____   _____

11. fähig _____   _____

12. überzeugt _____   _____

13. neidisch _____   _____

14. stolz _____   _____

15. froh _____   _____

Übung	20-2

Rewrite each sentence, completing it with the correct form of the phrase in parentheses.

1. Ist Gudrun zufrieden mit _____?

   a. (ihr Aufsatz) _____

   b. (ihre Brille) _____

   c. (ihre neuen Schuhe) _____

2. Der Lehrer war sehr böse auf _____ .

   a. (die ganze Klasse)   _____

   b. (der faule Schüler)   _____

   c. (diese Jungen)   _____

3. Ich bin noch nicht von _____ überzeugt.

   a. (deine Theorie)   _____

   b. (Ihre Ideen)   _____

   c. (dieser Plan)   _____

4. Der Richter ist mit _____ bekannt.

   a. (viele Politiker)   _____

   b. (der Bürgermeister)   _____

   c. (meine jüngste Tochter)   _____

5. Frau Keller ist sehr stolz auf _____ .

   a. (ihre Kinder)   _____

   b. (diese Studentin)   _____

   c. (unser Fortschritt)   _____

Übung 20-3

Complete each sentence, filling in the blank with any appropriate word or phrase.

1. Das Kind ist noch nicht fähig zu _____ .

2. Meine Schwester ist wieder böse auf _____ .

3. Wir müssen auf _____ aufmerksam sein.

4. Hans ist jetzt ganz fertig mit _____ .

5. Der berühmte Künstler war verliebt in _____ .

6. Wird Klaudia neidisch auf _____ sein?

7. Mein Großvater ist nicht mit _____ zufrieden.

8. Der Hauptmann scheint niemals stolz auf _____ zu sein.

9. Meine Kusine ist mit _____ bekannt.

10. Deutschland ist reich an _____.

Übung 20·4

Circle the preposition that best completes each sentence.

1. Ich bin nicht _____ ihre Stimme gewöhnt. an | auf | vor

2. Erik ist verliebt _____ Maria. für | von | in

3. Der junge Manager ist freundlich _____ dem Rechtsanwalt. zu | bei | aus

4. Wir waren glücklich _____ seinen Erfolg. über | bis | neben

5. Ich bin noch nicht _____ Frau Bauer bekannt. mit | unter | zu

6. Der Vater ist sehr stolz _____ die Kinder. auf | aus | an

7. Sie sind sehr neidisch _____ meine Schwester. durch | auf | seit

8. Karl war dankbar _____ meine Hilfe. ohne | mit | für

9. Bist du wieder böse _____ uns? auf | aus | von

10. Ich bin endlich _____ deiner Arbeit überzeugt. vor | bis | von

Prepositions as Prefixes

Many separable-verb prefixes are prepositions. They can be dative prepositions, accusative prepositions, accusative-dative prepositions, or even genitive prepositions. Separable prefixes are those that separate from the verb in the present, past, and perfect tenses. The following sentences show the conjugation of **ankommen** (**kommen** with the prefix **an-**) in the third-person singular in several tenses.

Er kommt **an**.	*He arrives.*
Er kam **an**.	*He arrived.*
Er ist **an**gekommen.	*He has arrived.*
Er war **an**gekommen.	*He had arrived.*
Er wird **an**kommen.	*He will arrive.*
Er wird **an**gekommen sein.	*He will have arrived.*

It is only in the future tense, where an infinitive is used with a conjugation of **werden**, that the prefix remains attached to the verb: **ankommen**. In the perfect tenses, the participle is separated from the prefix by **-ge-**: **angekommen**.

Accusative Prepositions as Prefixes

The common accusative prepositions are **bis**, **durch**, **für**, **gegen**, **ohne**, **um**, and **wider**. All of these prepositions can be used as prefixes, some to a greater extent than others.

Bis is used but rarely as a prefix. It is attached to a few adverbs and adjectives to form new words.

bisherig (*adjective*)	*until now, prevailing*
bisher (*adverb*)	*until now*
bislang (*adverb*)	*so far*
bisweilen (*adverb*)	*sometimes, occasionally*

Durch, on the other hand, is used in several ways as a prefix. It can be part of a noun, verb, adjective, or adverb.

der Durchbruch (*noun*)	*breakthrough*
der Durchgang (*noun*)	*passageway*

durchfrieren (*verb*)	*to become chilled through*
durchschlafen (*verb*)	*to sleep through*
durchdringlich (*adjective*)	*penetrating*
durchlässig (*adjective*)	*porous*
durchaus (*adverb*)	*throughout, completely*
durcheinander (*adverb*)	*in confusion*

Für is used as a prefix with a few nouns.

der Fürsorger / die Fürsorgerin (*noun*)	*welfare worker*
das Fürwort (*noun*)	*pronoun*

Gegen is used as a prefix with a variety of words.

der Gegensatz (*noun*)	*contrast*
die Gegenwirkung (*noun*)	*reaction*
gegensätzlich (*adjective*)	*contrary*
gegenwärtig (*adjective*)	*present*
gegeneinander (*adverb*)	*against one another*
gegenüber (*adverb, preposition*)	*opposite*

Ohne is rarely used as a prefix.

ohnegleichen (*adjective*)	*unequalled*
ohnehin (*adverb*)	*besides, anyway*

Um is used as a prefix for numerous nouns and verbs; the list is quite long, and only a few examples are given here.

der Umfang (*noun*)	*circumference, periphery*
der Umlaut (*noun*)	*vowel modification, umlaut*
umsteigen (*verb*)	*to transfer* (transportation)
umkippen (*verb*)	*to tip over*

Wider is also widely used as a prefix, generally with nouns, verbs, and adjectives.

der Widerhall (*noun*)	*echo*
der Widerspruch (*noun*)	*contradiction*
widerrufen (*verb*)	*to retract*
widerspiegeln (*verb*)	*to reflect*
widerlich (*adjective*)	*offensive*
widersprechend (*adjective*)	*contradictory*

Dative Prepositions as Prefixes

The common dative prepositions are **aus**, **außer**, **bei**, **gegenüber**, **mit**, **nach**, **seit**, **von**, and **zu**. Like accusative prepositions, some dative prepositions are used extensively as prefixes, and others not so widely.

Aus is used as a prefix with a large number of nouns and verbs. Adjectives derived from nouns and verbs with the **aus-** prefix are also prevalent.

die Auskunft (*noun*)	*information*
die Ausnahme (*noun*)	*exception*
ausdrücken (*verb*)	*to express*
ausziehen (*verb*)	*to undress*

| auserlesen (*adjective*) | *select, choice* |
| ausführlich (*adjective*) | *detailed* |

Außer is used as a prefix with a large number of adjectives and adverbs.

außerordentlich (*adjective*)	*extraordinary*
außerdienstlich (*adjective*)	*private, social*
außerdem (*adverb*)	*besides*
außerhalb (*adverb, preposition*)	*on the outside, outside*

Bei is used as a preposition with a large number of nouns and verbs. It also acts as a prefix with a small number of adverbs.

der Beifall (*noun*)	*applause*
die Beihilfe (*noun*)	*assistance*
beibringen (*verb*)	*to teach*
beistehen (*verb*)	*to stand by*
beinahe (*adverb*)	*almost*
beiseite (*adverb*)	*aside, apart*

Gegenüber is a combination of two prepositions, **gegen** and **über**. As a single preposition, **gegenüber** requires a dative case object. As a prefix, it combines with only a few words and is often used in a present participle form as a noun.

die Gegenüberstellung (*noun*)	*opposition*
gegenüberliegend (*adjective*)	*opposite*
gegenüberstehend (*adjective*)	*opposite*

Mit is used as a prefix with a wide variety of nouns and verbs, but also serves as a prefix with a number of adjectives.

das Mitglied (*noun*)	*member*
der/das Mittag (*noun*)	*noon; lunch*
mitbringen (*verb*)	*to bring along*
mitarbeiten (*verb*)	*to work together*
mitschuldig (*adjective*)	*implicated*
mitleidig (*adjective*)	*sympathetic*

Nach is used as a prefix with a very long list of words, including nouns, verbs, adjectives, and adverbs.

die Nachricht (*noun*)	*news*
der Nachtisch (*noun*)	*dessert*
nachahmen (*verb*)	*to imitate*
nachprüfen (*verb*)	*to check*
nachdrücklich (*adjective*)	*emphatic*
nachgelassen (*adjective*)	*unpublished*
nacheinander (*adverb*)	*after one another*
nachher (*adverb*)	*afterwards*

Seit functions as a prefix only rarely.

seitherig (*adjective*)	*subsequent*
seitdem (*adverb*)	*since then*
seither (*adverb*)	*from that time*

Von, likewise, has limited use as a prefix.

voneinander gehen (*verb*)	*to part company*
voneinander (*adverb*)	*from one another*
vonseiten (*preposition*)	*from the side of*

Zu as a prefix combines with many nouns, verbs, adjectives, and adverbs.

der Zufall (*noun*)	*chance, coincidence*
die Zunahme (*noun*)	*increase*
zugeben (*verb*)	*to admit*
zubleiben (*verb*)	*to remain shut*
zufrieden (*adjective*)	*satisfied*
zukünftig (*adjective*)	*future*
zuerst (*adverb*)	*at first*
zugute (*adverb*)	*to the benefit of*

Accusative-Dative Prepositions as Prefixes

The common accusative-dative prepositions are **an**, **auf**, **hinter**, **in**, **neben**, **über**, **unter**, **vor**, and **zwischen**.

An has many uses as a prefix and combines with nouns, verbs, adjectives, and adverbs.

die Ankunft (*noun*)	*arrival*
das Angeld (*noun*)	*earnest money*
ankommen (*verb*)	*to arrive*
ansehen (*verb*)	*to look at*
anlockend (*adjective*)	*attractive*
annehmbar (*adjective*)	*acceptable*
aneinander (*adverb*)	*at one another*
angriffsweise (*adverb*)	*aggressively*

Auf functions as a prefix with a very large number of nouns, verbs, and adjectives.

der Aufsatz (*noun*)	*article*
der Aufzug (*noun*)	*procession*
aufhören (*verb*)	*to stop*
aufmachen (*verb*)	*to open*
auflösbar (*adjective*)	*soluble*
aufdringlich (*adjective*)	*obtrusive*

Hinter is used as a prefix with a large number of words.

der Hintergedanke (*noun*)	*ulterior motive*
das Hinterhaus (*noun*)	*rear premises*
hintergehen (*verb*)	*to walk to the rear*
hinterlistig (*adjective*)	*deceitful*
hinterhältig (*adjective*)	*underhanded*
hinterher (*adverb*)	*behind*

Ein is the prefix form for the preposition **in**. This prefix is widely used with nouns, verbs, and adjectives.

der Eingang (*noun*)	*entrance*
die Einheit (*noun*)	*unity*
einfüllen (*verb*)	*to fill in*
einlösen (*verb*)	*to ransom, redeem*
einfarbig (*adjective*)	*of one color*
einförmig (*adjective*)	*uniform*

Neben is used as a prefix with a large number of nouns. Its use with verbs, adjectives, and adverbs is rare.

die Nebenfrage (*noun*)	*secondary issue*
die Nebenperson (*noun*)	*subordinate*
nebeneinanderstellen (*verb*)	*to compare*
nebenständig (*adjective*)	*accessory*
nebeneinander (*adverb*)	*next to one another*

Über is used as a prefix with a large number of nouns, verbs, adjectives, and adverbs.

der Überfluss (*noun*)	*abundance*
der Übermensch (*noun*)	*superman*
überhängen (*verb*)	*to hang over*
übernehmen (*verb*)	*to take delivery of*
überglücklich (*adjective*)	*extremely happy*
übernatürlich (*adjective*)	*supernatural*
überhaupt (*adverb*)	*generally*
übernacht (*adverb*)	*overnight*

Unter is used primarily as a prefix with nouns and verbs. There are a few adjectives and adverbs that also use this prefix.

der Untergrund (*noun*)	*foundation*
der Unterhändler (*noun*)	*negotiator*
unterbrechen (*verb*)	*to interrupt*
unterbringen (*verb*)	*to shelter*
unterbewusst (*adjective*)	*subconscious*
untereinander (*adverb*)	*between each other*

Vor is another prefix that is widely used with nouns, verbs, adjectives, and adverbs.

das Vorgefühl (*noun*)	*foreboding*
die Vorsicht (*noun*)	*precaution*
vorbereiten (*verb*)	*to prepare*
vorgehen (*verb*)	*to run too fast* (clock)
vorbildlich (*adjective*)	*typical*
vorehelich (*adjective*)	*prenuptial*
im Voraus (*adverb*)	*in advance*
vorbei (*adverb*)	*past*

Zwischen is used as a prefix primarily with nouns.

die Zwischenbemerkung (*noun*)	*aside*
das Zwischengericht (*noun*)	*side dish*
die Zwischenlandung (*noun*)	*touchdown, stopover*
die Zwischenstation (*noun*)	*intermediate stage/station*

Genitive Prepositions as Prefixes

The four most common genitive prepositions are **(an)statt**, **trotz**, **während**, and **wegen**.

Statt is used as a prefix with a small number of nouns, verbs, and adjectives. The form **anstatt** is never used as a prefix.

der Statthalter (*noun*)	*governor*
die Stattlichkeit (*noun*)	*elegance*
stattgeben (*verb*)	*to allow*
stattfinden (*verb*)	*to take place*
statthaft (*adjective*)	*admissible*
stattlich (*adjective*)	*imposing*

Trotz as a prefix is used with a very small number of words.

das Trotzalter (*noun*)	*difficult age*
der Trotzkopf (*noun*)	*stubborn person*
trotzig (*adjective*)	*defiant*

Während is used as a prefix with the adverb **währenddessen** (*meanwhile*).

Wegen is never used as a prefix.

Preposition Combinations

Sometimes two prepositions combine to form a new prefix. These combinations are not influenced by the case required by the prepositions. For example, the prefix **vorbei-** is composed of the accusative-dative preposition **vor** and the dative preposition **bei**. Other examples follow.

durchaus (*adverb*)	*throughout*
die Gegenanklage (*noun*)	*countercharge*
überaus (*adverb*)	*exceedingly*
vorbeikommen (*verb*)	*to drop by*
zuvor (*adverb*)	*previously*

Knowing the meaning of a preposition is often helpful in determining the meaning of a word to which it is prefixed. The preposition **trotz**, for example, means *despite* or *in spite of*. When this word forms an adjective, it becomes **trotzig**. Based on the meaning of the preposition, one might guess that the adjective means *spiteful*—close to the word's meaning, *defiant*.

As another example, the preposition **vor** (*before, in front of*) combines with **Gefühl** (*feeling*) to become **Vorgefühl**. One might guess that it means *a feeling before some event*, or *a foreboding*.

Although this kind of word analysis doesn't yield perfect results, it is a useful way to get the gist of a word when a dictionary is not nearby.

Übung	21-1

Fill in each blank with the missing prefix so that the meaning of the new word coincides with the English translation given.

1. _____ mensch   *superman*

2. _____ gehen   *to walk to the rear*

3. _____ her   *until now*

4. _____ bruch   *breakthrough*

5. _____ sprechen   *to speak on someone's behalf*

6. _____ ehelich   *prenuptial*

7. _____ bewusst   *subconscious*

8. _____ zug   *procession*

9. _____ brechen   *interrupt*

10. _____ natürlich   *supernatural*

11. _____ frage   *secondary issue*

12. _____ förmig   *uniform*

13. _____ gang   *entrance*

14. _____ einander   *at one another*

15. _____ station   *intermediate stage*

Forming New Words

German forms many new words by using prefixes, and a large number of those prefixes are prepositions. A single noun or verb can generate numerous new nouns or verbs with the addition of prefixes. This can sometimes be problematic for students of German, because knowing the meaning of the *base noun* or *verb* does not necessarily mean that it has the same meaning when it has a prefix. Most students know that **kommen** means *to come.* But **verkommen** has a very distinct meaning from the base verb—it means *to go bad.* It's important not to jump to conclusions about the meaning of a prefixed word just because you know the meaning of the base word.

Some prefixes combined with a noun or verb are more easily understood than others. The meaning of **durch** and **mit**, for example, is often quite clear.

durchfahren	*to drive through*
durchlesen	*to read through*
mitkommen	*to come along*
mitsingen	*to sing along*

Prefixes often give a clue to the meaning of a word, but it is wise to consult a dictionary to be sure of its meaning. Still, it is important not to underestimate the importance of prefixes.

Some of the prefixes in the following chart are inseparable verb prefixes, and others come from prepositions.

die Ankunft	*arrival*	aufschlagen	*to open*
die Auskunft	*information*	nachschlagen	*to look up* (a word)
die Zukunft	*future*	zuschlagen	*to slam shut*
die Ansicht	*sight*	annehmen	*to assume*
die Aussicht	*view*	abnehmen	*to reduce*
besichtigen	*to go sightseeing*	die Zunahme	*increase*
gehören	*to belong (to)*	der Anspruch	*demand*
aufhören	*to stop*	versprechen	*to promise*
das Verhör	*interrogation*	entsprechen	*to correspond (to)*
ertrinken	*to drown*	beschreiben	*to describe*
austrinken	*to finish drinking*	die Anschrift	*address*
das Getränk	*beverage*	die Unterschrift	*signature*

The following charts show how prefixes affect the meaning of some verbs of motion.

	kommen		**fahren**	
ab	abkommen	*to get away*	abfahren	*to depart by transportation*
an	ankommen	*to arrive*	anfahren	*to drive up to*
aus	auskommen	*to make do*	ausfahren	*to take for a drive*
be	bekommen	*to receive*	befahren	*to travel over*
durch	durchkommen	*to come through*	durchfahren	*to drive through*
ent	entkommen	*to escape*	entfahren	*to slip out*
mit	mitkommen	*to come along*	mitfahren	*to drive along*
um	umkommen	*to die*	umfahren	*to run over*
ver	verkommen	*to decay*	das Verfahren	*procedure*
vor	vorkommen	*to come forward*	vorfahren	*to drive up to*
weg	wegkommen	*to come away*	wegfahren	*to cart away*
zu	die Zukunft	*future*	die Zufahrt	*driveway*

	fliegen		**reisen**	
ab	abfliegen	*to fly off*	abreisen	*to depart*
an	anfliegen	*to fly to*	anreisen	*to arrive*
aus	Ausflug	*outing*	Ausreise	*journey abroad*
durch	durchfliegen	*to fly through*	durchreisen	*to travel through*
ent	entfliegen	*to fly away*	—	
mit	mitfliegen	*to fly along*	mitreisen	*to journey together*
um	umfliegen	*to fly around*	umreisen	*to travel around*
ver	verfliegen	*to fly the wrong way*	verreisen	*to go on a trip*
weg	wegfliegen	*to fly away*	wegreisen	*to set out on a journey*
zu	zufliegen	*to slam shut*	—	

The patterns of meaning with prefixes will help you discover the meaning of new words. It is important to be aware that the same prefix used with a noun, verb, or even an adjective derived from the same base word can produce varied meanings. For example, the following three words are derived from the verb **sprechen** and are prefixed with **an**.

ansprechen (*verb*)	*to address*
der Anspruch (*noun*)	*demand*
anspruchsvoll (*adjective*)	*pretentious*

With verbs of motion, it is very common to use the prefixes **an-** and **ab-** to mean *arrival* and *departure* or a similar meaning.

ankommen	*to arrive*
abkommen	*to go astray*
anfahren	*to run into*
abfahren	*to depart*
anreisen	*to travel there*
abreisen	*to depart*

The most important concept to understand in this unit is that prefixes play a significant role in the German language. Various prefixes can provide nuances of meaning for a single verb or produce identical or similar changes in the meaning of a variety of verbs. Knowing how prefixes function will give you the skill to speak and understand German at a much higher level.

Übung   21-2

Fill in each blank with the missing prefix so that the meaning of the new word coincides with the English translation given.

1. _____ reisen   *to travel through*

2. _____ hören   *to stop*

3. _____ singen   *to sing along*

4. _____ lesen   *to read through*

5. _____ kommen   *to arrive*

6. _____ fahren   *to drive through*

7. _____ fliegen   *to fly along*

8. _____ schrift   *signature*

9. _____ trinken   *to finish drinking*

10. _____ sicht   *view*

Prepositional Contractions

Some German prepositions combine with definite articles that follow to form contractions. While the list of these contractions is not long, they are important because they are used frequently in spoken language and are also found in written language. These contractions are formed with definite articles in the dative and accusative cases only.

Six contractions are formed with five different prepositions and the dative case of the singular definite article. Notice that only one feminine dative definite article can form a contraction.

an dem	**am**
in dem	**im**
bei dem	**beim**
von dem	**vom**
zu dem	**zum**
zu der	**zur**

These contractions are used in sentences in place of the preposition and article, but have no effect on the grammar of the sentence.

> Bist du wieder **am** Telefon?
> *Are you on the phone again?*

> Meine Mutter ist noch **im** Büro.
> *My mother is still at the office.*

> Karl wohnt **beim** Onkel.
> *Karl lives at his uncle's house.*

> Sie kommen gleich **vom** Theater.
> *They're coming from the theater now.*

> Wir laufen **zum** Stadtpark.
> *We run to the city park.*

> Willst du **zur** Schule gehen?
> *Do you want to go to school?*

Other contractions are formed from prepositions with the accusative case of the neuter singular definite article.

an das	**ans**
auf das	**aufs**
für das	**fürs**
in das	**ins**
um das	**ums**

Contractions are merely shorter versions of the original preposition and definite article, and have no effect on the grammar of the sentence.

Die Kinder gehen **ans** Fenster.
The children go to the window.

Der Bauer kehrt wieder **aufs** Land.
The farmer returns to the country.

Inge dankt Erich **fürs** Geschenk.
Inge thanks Erich for the gift.

Die Katze lief **ins** Wohnzimmer.
The cat ran into the living room.

Sie trauern **ums** Kind.
They're in mourning over the child.

Übung   22-1

In each blank write the contraction for the preposition + definite article. If the combination cannot form a contraction, write an X.

1. von der   _____
2. auf das   _____
3. an das   _____
4. zu dem   _____
5. zu der   _____
6. unter den   _____
7. für das   _____
8. in dem   _____
9. um das   _____
10. auf den   _____
11. in das   _____

12. bei dem   _____

13. von dem   _____

14. aus dem   _____

15. an den   _____

Übung	22-2

Write original sentences, using the contractions in parentheses.

1. (im)   _____

2. (ins)   _____

3. (vom)   _____

4. (aufs) _____

5. (zum)   _____

6. (zur)   _____

7. (ums)   _____

8. (am)   _____

9. (ans)   _____

10. (beim) _____

Review Exercises

By now you should be well acquainted with German pronouns and prepositions. Use the following exercises as a review of pronouns and prepositions and as a check of your accurate usage of them.

Pronouns

Fill in the blank with the appropriate subject pronoun.

    EXAMPLE   Das ist Herr Braun. __*Er*__ wohnt in der Schillerstraße.

1. _____ habe keine Zeit.

2. Karl und ich lernen Spanisch. _____ wollen nach Madrid reisen.

3. Kannst _____ diese Sätze übersetzen?

4. Kinder, _____ müsst jetzt nach Hause kommen.

5. _____ ist meine Großmutter.

6. Diese Stühle sind nicht neu. _____ sind alt.

7. Frau Keller, _____ haben Ihren Regenschirm vergessen.

8. Das ist Sabine. _____ ist eine Freundin von mir.

9. _____ bin sechs Jahre älter als mein Bruder.

10. _____ hat ein neues Fahrrad von seinen Eltern bekommen.

11. _____ war sehr kalt und windig.

12. Habt _____ ihm damit geholfen?

13. Ich habe Durst, aber _____ gibt keine Milch mehr.

14. Der BMW ist alt, aber _____ fährt noch gut.

15. Kennst du Werner und Angela? _____ sind Österreicher.

Übung	R-2

Circle the letter of the word or words that best replace the pronoun in boldface.

1. **Er** ist ein Freund von mir.
   - a. Frau Benz
   - b. Der Rechtsanwalt
   - c. Tina
   - d. Diese Leute

2. **Sie** hat ihre Tasche wieder verloren.
   - a. Eine Schauspielerin
   - b. Herr Keller
   - c. Martin und Sabine
   - d. Keine Damen

3. **Es** schläft auf dem Sofa.
   - a. Das Kind
   - b. Unsere Großmutter
   - c. Meine Eltern
   - d. Der Lehrer

4. **Wir** denken oft an euch.
   - a. Diese Jungen
   - b. Rolf und seine Schwester
   - c. Die neue Studentin
   - d. Meine Brüder und ich

5. Sind **sie** noch in der Hauptstadt?
   - a. deine Kusine
   - b. deine Söhne
   - c. Ihr Onkel
   - d. Ihre Verwandten

6. **Es** kostet nur zehn Euro.
   - a. Diese Zeitungen
   - b. Diese Zeitung
   - c. Diese Bücher
   - d. Dieses Buch

7. **Sie** müssen sofort nach Hause gehen.
   - a. Die kleinsten Kinder
   - b. Mein Vetter
   - c. Eure Tante
   - d. Unsere neue Lehrerin

8. **Sie** ist eine Nonne.
   - a. Maria
   - b. Sonja und Angelika
   - c. Diese Frauen
   - d. Ein Mädchen

9. **Er** ist kaputt.
   a. Der neue Fernsehapparat
   b. Dieses Auto
   c. Eine alte Waschmaschine
   d. Kein Fenster

10. **Er** arbeitet als Juwelier.
   a. Seine Kollegin
   b. Meine Freunde
   c. Seine Enkelin
   d. Mein Neffe

Übung   R-3

Fill in the blank with the appropriate present tense conjugation of the verb in parentheses.

> EXAMPLE   Er __*kommt*__ mit seinem Bruder. (kommen)

1. Er _____ lange. (schlafen)

2. _____ sie deine Großmutter? (sein)

3. Wir _____ keine Zeit. (haben)

4. Wo sind die Kinder? Sie _____ im Garten. (spielen)

5. Endlich _____ sie sich einen Mann. (nehmen)

6. Es _____ sehr heiß. (werden)

7. _____ du Fußball oder Tennis spielen? (können)

8. Ich _____ heute zu Hause bleiben. (müssen)

9. _____ ihr ins Theater gehen? (wollen)

10. Das ist Angela. Sie _____ gut Deutsch. (sprechen)

Übung   R-4

Fill in the blank with the pronoun in the accusative case that correctly replaces the noun or phrase in boldface.

> EXAMPLE   Ich kenne den Herrn nicht. __*ihn*__

1. Ich habe **Gerhardt Schmidt** in Kanada kennengelernt. _____

2. Wo hast du **mein Heft** gefunden? _____

3. Er hat **die neue Vase** auf dem Tisch stehen gelassen. _____

4. Wir haben **den Zug** verpasst! _____

5. Wer kann **dieses Problem** lösen? _____

6. Mutter hat **meinen Regenmantel** im Keller gefunden. _____

7. Der Blitz hat **zwei Pferde** getötet. _____

8. Martin wird **eine weiße Nelke** kaufen. _____

9. Ich liebe **das schöne Wetter**. _____

10. Onkel Karl hat **den Schlüssel** versteckt. _____

11. Wirst du **Thomas und mich** besuchen? _____

12. Im Sommer werden wir **unsere Verwandten** in New York besuchen. _____

13. Ich kenne **das Mädchen** nicht. _____

14. Gudrun hat **die Fragen** zu langsam beantwortet. _____

15. Kannst du **ihre Handschrift** lesen? _____

Übung   R-5

Circle the letter of the noun or pronoun that is the appropriate replacement for the word or phrase in boldface.

EXAMPLE   **Der Lehrer** ist spät angekommen.
a. Er
b. Sie
c. Wir
d. Euch

1. **Solche Umstände** ärgern mich.
a. Ihr
b. Euch
c. Sie
d. Uns

2. Mein Vetter kennt **ihn** nicht.
a. eure Freunde
b. diesen Mann
c. ein kleines Kind
d. ihr Bruder

3. Martin kaufte **das Geschenk** für seine Schwester.

   a. ihr
   b. sie
   c. es
   d. ihn

4. **Sie** hat seit ihrer Jugend Sport getrieben.

   a. Ihre Schwester
   b. Die jungen Sportler
   c. Ein Freund von mir
   d. Eure Bekannten

5. **Der Arbeitslose** verdient nichts.

   a. Uns
   b. Er
   c. Ich
   d. Sie

6. **Wir** treffen sie am Hauptbahnhof.

   a. Viele Leute
   b. Karin und ich
   c. Sie
   d. Niemand

7. Meine Tante hat **den Pförtner** gefragt.

   a. ihn
   b. ihm
   c. ihnen
   d. Ihnen

8. Ich liebe **meine Heimat** am meisten.

   a. er
   b. ihn
   c. es
   d. sie

9. **Seinen Bruder** haben wir in London gesehen.

   a. Er
   b. Sie
   c. Ihn
   d. Ihm

10. Ich werde **meinen Urlaub** in Innsbruck verleben.

    a. es
    b. uns
    c. mich
    d. ihn

Übung   R-6

Change the noun in the prepositional phrase to a pronoun, and rewrite the prepositional phrase either with that pronoun or as a prepositional adverb.

EXAMPLE   ohne den Mann ___*ohne ihn*___

mit dem Buch ___*damit*___

1. ohne seine Geschwister _____

2. um das Kind _____

3. für eine Briefmarke _____

4. um die Ecke _____

5. ohne Martin _____

6. durch das Fenster _____

7. ohne ihre Schwester _____

8. gegen den Strom _____

9. für diesen Herrn _____

10. durch einen Tunnel _____

Übung   R-7

Change the noun or phrase in boldface either to the appropriate pronoun in the dative case or to a prepositional adverb.

EXAMPLE   Sie glaubt **meinem Freund** nicht. ___*ihm*___

1. Ich habe **meiner Freundin** dafür gedankt. _____

2. Sein Freund hat **mit Gudrun** getanzt. _____

3. Was hat sie **den Kindern** gegeben? _____

4. Morgen fahren wir **zu unseren Verwandten**. _____

5. Ihr Ring ist **aus Gold**. _____

6. Tante Gerda hat **ihrer Tochter** ein Geschenk geschickt. _____

7. Es gehört nicht **diesem Mädchen**. _____

8. **Nach der Party** gingen wir ins Kino. _____

9. Haben Sie lange **bei deiner Tante** gewohnt? _____

10. Der Anzug passt **Ihrem Sohn** gar nicht. _____

11. Wer hat **deinen Schwestern** die Blumen geschenkt? _____

12. Alle sprechen **von der neuen Schülerin**. _____

13. Die Würstchen schmecken **den Männern** nicht. _____

14. Sie spricht nicht **mit Karl und mir**. _____

15. Martin kommt **von der Bank**. _____

Übung   R-8

Fill in the blank with the pronoun that appropriately replaces the noun phrase in boldface. Note that the nouns and phrases are in the nominative, the accusative, or the dative case.

EXAMPLE   Mein Onkel spricht mit **der Lehrerin**. __*ihr*__

1. Die Frau gibt **dem Kind** eine Münze. _____

2. Karl hat **einen neuen Anzug** gekauft. _____

3. Die Jungen wollen mit **der Spanierin** tanzen. _____

4. Wir haben **ein Paket** von einem alten Freund bekommen. _____

5. Wem wird **Herr Weber** das Fahrrad geben? _____

6. Ich wohne lieber bei **meinem Bruder**. _____

7. Brauchst du **diese Bücher** nicht? _____

8. Ich werde nie gegen **meinen Vater** sprechen. _____

9. **Herr Benz** arbeitet seit Januar in Amerika. _____

10. Die Reiseleiterin hat **das Gemälde** den Touristen gezeigt. _____

11. Der Rundfunk teilt **ihrer Großmutter** die Nachrichten mit. _____

12. Kannst du **deinen Nachbarn** damit helfen? _____

13. Warum soll ich **diesem Fremden** glauben? _____

14. Erik hat **seinem Onkel** für das Geschenk gedankt. _____

15. **Sein Auto** ist wieder kaputt. _____

Übung   R-9

Write out the possessive adjective form of the following pronouns.

1. ich   _____

2. du   _____

3. er   _____

4. sie (*sing.*)   _____

5. es   _____

6. wir   _____

7. ihr   _____

8. sie (*pl.*)   _____

9. Sie   _____

10. wer   _____

Übung   R-10

Change the accusative or dative object in boldface to either the accusative or dative reflexive pronoun.

EXAMPLE   Er wäscht **seinem Bruder** das Gesicht. __*sich*__

1. Ich will **euch** ein Spiel kaufen. _____

2. Warum müsst ihr **der Lehrerin** widersprechen? _____

3. Herr Kaufmann hat **die Katze** auf einen Stuhl gesetzt. _____

4. Mutter fragt **Vater**, was geschehen ist. _____

5. Erik putzte **dem kleinsten Kind** die Zähne. _____

6. Die älteren Kinder helfen **den anderen**, so gut sie können. _____

7. Wir kämmen **ihm** die Haare. _____

8. Du hast **mich** schon überzeugt. _____

9. Der wahnsinnige Mann hat **sie** getötet. _____

10. Hast du **deiner Freundin** ein Geburtstagsgeschenk gefunden? _____

Prepositions

Übung   R-11

Rewrite each of the words or phrases in parentheses as they should appear following the accusative preposition.

    EXAMPLE   Er arbeitet für _____.

        (dein Bruder)   *deinen Bruder*

        (seine Schwester)   *seine Schwester*

1. Sie kann nicht gegen _____ sprechen.

    (seine Kinder) _____

    (ihr älterer Bruder) _____

2. Der Chef handelt ohne _____.

    (jede Rücksicht auf uns) _____

    (Vernunft) _____

3. Unsere Gäste können bis _____ bleiben.

    (Montag) _____

    (nächste Woche) _____

4. Ich werde mich immer um _____ bemühen.

    (meine Familie) _____

    (mein Sohn) _____

5. Ein kleiner Vogel ist durch _____ geflogen.

    (das Haus) _____

    (der große Lesesaal) _____

Übung   R-12

Fill in the blank with the preposition **für**, **bis**, or **um**, as appropriate.

1. Ich war oft _____ meine Eltern besorgt.

2. Er geht mit uns _____ an das Ende der Straße.

3. Hat er euch _____ das nette Geschenk gedankt?

4. Diese Arbeit ist typisch _____ einen Achtjährigen.

5. Kommt ihr _____ vierzehn Uhr?

Übung   R-13

Rewrite each of the words or phrases in parentheses as they should appear following the dative preposition.

    EXAMPLE   Zwei Vögel fliegen aus _____.

                (das Fenster) _*dem Fenster*_

                (ein Tunnel) _*einem Tunnel*_

1. Alle fragen nach _____.

    (meine Mutter) _____

    (unsere Kinder) _____

2. Wie lange werden Sie bei _____ wohnen?

    (Ihre Tante) _____

    (ein Bekannter) _____

3. Seid ihr mit _____ zufrieden?

    (dieses Zimmer) _____

    (der neue Manager) _____

4. Das jüngste Kind ist sehr verschieden von _____.

    (sein Vater) _____

    (seine Brüder) _____

5. Heute abend gehen wir zu _____.

(er) _____

(Sie) _____

Übung   R-14

Rewrite each of the words or phrases in parentheses as they should appear following prepositions that can take either the accusative or dative case.

EXAMPLE   Die Jungen arbeiten in _*dem Garten*_. (der Garten)

1. Eine Fledermaus ist zwischen _____ geflogen. (die Häuser)

2. Wir wollen neben _____ sitzen. (er)

3. Der bellende Hund läuft an _____. (das offene Fenster)

4. Warum legst du meine Sachen auf _____? (der Boden)

5. Warum hast du dich hinter _____ versteckt? (die Tür)

6. Herr Schäfer wohnt jetzt in _____ von Berlin. (ein Vorort)

7. Der weinende Junge ist oben auf _____. (das Dach)

8. Ich habe es unter _____ gefunden. (jener Tisch)

9. Wir sind in _____ gleich wieder da. (fünf Minuten)

10. Ich werde meinen Regenmantel in _____ hängen. (der Schrank)

Übung   R-15

Rewrite each of the words or phrases in parentheses as they should appear following the genitive preposition.

EXAMPLE   Er ist wegen _____ bei uns geblieben.

(eine Krankheit) _*einer Krankheit*_

(das Wetter) _*des Wetters*_

1. Während _____ musst du zu Hause bleiben.

(ein Gewitter) _____

(ein Schneesturm) _____

2. Anstatt _____ befindet sich in der Schublade ein Bleistift.

(ihre Ohrringe) _____

(meine Brille) _____

3. Trotz _____ kommt er jeden Tag zur Arbeit.

(seine Krankheit) _____

(der Unfall) _____

4. Wir sind wegen _____ in Sorge.

(unsere Kinder) _____

(unser Problem) _____

5. Jenseits _____ sahen wir eine alte Burg.

(der Fluss) _____

(die Berge) _____

6. Nur innerhalb _____ wird darüber gesprochen.

(seine Familie) _____

(die Partei) _____

7. Während _____ musste ich daran arbeiten.

(der ganze Tag) _____

(die ersten zwei Stunden) _____

8. Statt _____ hat er uns eine Ansichtskarte geschickt.

(ein Geschenk) _____

(ein langer Brief) _____

9. Ich kann wegen _____ leider nicht kommen.

(eine Erkältung) _____

(der Tod meiner Großmutter) _____

10. Trotz _____ sind wir an die Front gefahren.

(der Krieg) _____

(seine Warnung) _____

Übung   **R-16**

Circle the letter of the preposition that best completes each sentence.

EXAMPLE   Ich habe lange _____ ihn gearbeitet.
  a. von
  (b.) für
  c. bis
  d. außerhalb

1. Die Kinder laufen _____ die Tür.
  a. an
  b. ins
  c. am
  d. im

2. Haben Sie schon _____ Herrn Weber gesprochen?
  a. nach
  b. während
  c. aus
  d. mit

3. Morgen fahren wir wieder _____ unserem Sohn.
  a. durch
  b. zu
  c. bei
  d. seit

4. Sie haben _____ des Wetters Verspätung.
  a. gegen
  b. auf
  c. wegen
  d. anstatt

5. Ein langer Zug kam _____ den Tunnel.
  a. durch
  b. von
  c. aus
  d. ins

6. Um wie viel Uhr fährt der Bus _____ Bremen?
   a. im
   b. außer
   c. nach
   d. hinter

7. Sie hat das Geld _____ dem Teppich versteckt.
   a. am
   b. bis
   c. unter
   d. während

8. Er kaufte einen Hut _____ eines Hemdes.
   a. bei
   b. gegen
   c. um
   d. statt

9. Sie hat ein Bild _____ die Wand gehängt.
   a. an
   b. von
   c. trotz
   d. durch

10. Jetzt kommen die Kinder _____ der Schule.
    a. wegen
    b. aus
    c. im
    d. auf

11. Wir wohnen _____ März in Heidelberg.
    a. seit
    b. bei
    c. zu
    d. zum

12. Die Mädchen laufen _____ Marktplatz.
    a. ins
    b. in
    c. zur
    d. zum

13. Warum steht die Stehlampe _____ dem Klavier?
    a. vor
    b. außer
    c. bis
    d. trotz

14. _____ wen wartet ihr?
   a. Auf
   b. Aus
   c. In
   d. Mit

15. Der Dichter lebte _____ zu seinem Tod in Bonn.
   a. von
   b. wegen
   c. bis
   d. an

Übung	R-17

Select the word or phrase in parentheses that best completes each sentence. Fill in the blank with that word or phrase in its appropriate form.

EXAMPLE   Meine Mutter kaufte __*mir*__ einen neuen Mantel. (ich, wegen, für)

1. Man _____ nicht fluchen. (brauchen, hatte, sollen)

2. Ich habe _____ vorgestellt. (trotz, er, nach)

3. Wann _____ du nach Hause? (kommen, wollen, dich)

4. Der Direktor hat nichts gegen _____. (du, wissen, durch)

5. Ich habe zwei Pullover. _____ magst du? (welcher, durch, wir)

6. Wir haben _____ in München getroffen. (sie, während, tun)

7. Ich habe ein Geschenk _____ euch. (sein, kaufen, für)

8. Wir haben _____ Freund besucht. (trotz, unser, auf)

9. Warum tanzt er nicht mit _____? (euer, ich, gehen)

10. Er musste _____ Wagen verkaufen. (machen, zu, sein)

11. Wie viele Fahrkarten hattest _____? (mein, gegen, du)

12. Sie _____ ein Glas Wein. (dürfen, von, bestellen)

13. Ich gab _____ ein paar Euro. (er, aus, mit)

14. Was hat er _____ geschickt? (Sie, zu, sollen)

15. Er _____ jetzt keine Zeit. (mögen, hinter, haben)

16. Frau Keller stellt es _____ die Tische. (aus, zwischen, wegen)

17. Alle _____ mir verstehen es. (ich, können, außer)

18. Karl hat _____ ihr geschenkt. (euer, es, während)

19. Wir bleiben wegen _____ zu Hause. (Schnee, bis, müssen)

20. Ein Spiegel hängt über _____. (nach, sollen, Klavier)

21. _____ gebt zu viel Geld aus. (ich, können, ihr)

22. Der Lehrer erkennt _____ nicht. (haben, sein, ich)

23. Wir steigen in _____ aus. (Hauptstraße, hinter, sollen)

24. _____ ist sehr kalt geworden. (können, es, Sie)

25. Erik kommt _____ dreizehn Uhr an. (Zug, von, um)

26. Ich habe drei Bücher. _____ willst du? (anstatt, welcher, man)

27. Er kaufte drei Uhren, aber _____ sind kaputt. (wessen, zwei, ohne)

28. Sind Sie zufrieden mit _____? (vor, der neue Anzug, aneinander)

29. Seine Eltern sind sehr stolz _____ ihn. (um, sich, auf)

30. Mein Vater gibt mir alles, _____ ich verlange. (was, mich, wen)

31. Die Kandidaten müssen _____ sitzen. (mit, nebeneinander, vor)

32. _____ nicht mein Freund ist, ist mein Feind. (er, trotz, wer)

33. Ihr Haus ist groß, aber _____ ist klein. (es, mein, viel)

34. Interessierst du _____ für Chemie? (du, Sie, ihr)

35. Wir können bis _____ den Fluss laufen. (zu, aus, an)

The Verb *Get* in German

The English verb *get* yields a wide variety of meanings, which depend on the phrase it is used in. Following is a list of uses of the verb *get*, with the prepositions that accompany it, as well as the German equivalent of each phrase. The meaning of the English preposition is often conveyed by a preposition or a prefix in German. Note that the verb **werden** is frequently, but not exclusively, a translation for *get*.

Get with a preposition	German equivalent
get into	eintreten
get into (vehicles)	einsteigen
get out of	austreten
get out of/off (vehicles)	aussteigen
get to	kommen zu/in
get from	kommen aus/von
get up	aufstehen
get down	heruntersteigen
get along with	auskommen mit

Prepositions and Their Required Cases

Accusative	Dative	Accusative-dative	Genitive
bis	aus	an	anstatt/statt
durch	außer	auf	angesichts
entlang	bei	hinter	anlässlich
für	gegenüber	in	außerhalb
gegen	mit	neben	beiderseits
ohne	nach	über	bezüglich
um	seit	unter	diesseits
wider	trotz	vor	hinsichtlich
	von	zwischen	innerhalb
	wegen		jenseits
	zu		oberhalb
			trotz
			unterhalb
			während
			wegen

Verbs That Require Specific Prepositions

antworten	auf
bedanken (sich)	bei
beklagen (sich)	bei
bekommen	von
beschäftigen (sich)	mit
bewerben (sich)	um
bezahlen	für
bitten	um
blicken	auf
denken	an
erzählen	von
fahren	mit, nach, zu
fliegen	mit, nach, zu
fragen	nach
freuen (sich)	auf, über
gehen	nach, zu
gehören	zu
hängen	an, über
interessieren (sich)	für
kämpfen	gegen
kommen	aus, von
laufen	nach, zu
reisen	mit, nach, zu
sein	aus
sprechen	über, von
suchen	nach
warten	auf
wohnen	bei

Answer Key

Part I Pronouns
Unit 1 Pronouns in the Nominative Case

1-1
1. Es hat lange geschlafen.
2. Ist sie deine Großmutter?
3. Er hat sich gestern das Bein gebrochen.
4. Sie kämpfen gegen das Schicksal.
5. Wo sind sie?
6. Sie wird den Ofen heizen.
7. Sie war mit dieser Arbeit zufrieden.
8. Sie wachsen nicht hier.
9. Hat er meinen Pullover genommen?
10. Es wohnt nicht weit von uns.

1-2
1. a. Ich begehe ein Verbrechen.
   b. Du begehst ein Verbrechen.
   c. Wir begehen ein Verbrechen.
   d. Ihr begeht ein Verbrechen.
2. a. Ich bin fertig zur Reise.
   b. Du bist fertig zur Reise.
   c. Wir sind fertig zur Reise.
   d. Ihr seid fertig zur Reise.
3. a. Ich borge dem Kaufmann Geld.
   b. Du borgst dem Kaufmann Geld.
   c. Wir borgen dem Kaufmann Geld.
   d. Ihr borgt dem Kaufmann Geld.
4. a. Ich habe die Fragen beantwortet.
   b. Du hast die Fragen beantwortet.
   c. Wir haben die Fragen beantwortet.
   d. Ihr habt die Fragen beantwortet.

1-3
1. a. Ich brachte die Bücher mit.
   b. Du brachtest die Bücher mit.
   c. Wir brachten die Bücher mit.
   d. Ihr brachtet die Bücher mit.
2. a. Ich wollte zu Hause bleiben.
   b. Du wolltest zu Hause bleiben.
   c. Wir wollten zu Hause bleiben.
   d. Ihr wolltet zu Hause bleiben.
3. a. Ich kaufte ein Haus in Freiburg.
   b. Du kauftest ein Haus in Freiburg.
   c. Wir kauften ein Haus in Freiburg.
   d. Ihr kauftet ein Haus in Freiburg.

1-4
These are sample answers only.
1. Der Manager ist ein Freund von mir.
2. Eine alte Frau hat ihre Tasche wieder verloren.
3. Das kranke Kind schläft auf dem Sofa.
4. Karin und ich denken oft an euch.
5. Sind die Reisenden noch in der Hauptstadt?

1-5

1. Was kostet nur zehn Euro?
2. Wer muss sofort nach Hause gehen?
3. Wer ist eine Nonne?
4. Was ist kaputt?
5. Wer arbeitet als Juwelier?

1-6

1. **Ich** bin wieder krank geworden.
2. **Wir** haben Onkel Heinrich besucht.
3. **Sie** (*pl.*) verstehen das nicht.
4. **Es** ist ziemlich kalt.
5. Geht **ihr** wieder aufs Land?
6. **Er** lässt uns im Stich.
7. **Sie** (*sing.*) hilft ihren Eltern.
8. **Ihr** habt eine großen Storch gesehen.
9. Hört **Erhardt** die Musik?
10. **Wir** können ein paar Sätze schreiben.
11. **Es** mag sein.
12. **Mein Vetter** kann Spanisch und Russisch.
13. Warum warst **du** im Krankenhaus?
14. **Das Schauspiel** war nicht so gut, wie wir erwartet hatten.
15. **Ich** habe gehorchen müssen.

Unit 2   Pronouns and Gender

2-1
1. chair, er
2. chalk, sie (*sing.*)
3. money, es
4. newspapers, sie (*pl.*)
5. people, sie (*pl.*)
6. guest, er
7. girlfriend, sie (*sing.*)
8. miss, es
9. athlete, er
10. racing car, er

2-2
1. Es ist ziemlich weit von hier.
2. Wo ist es?
3. Sie ist nur noch ein Traum.
4. Sie ist sehr krank geworden.
5. Kann er Klavier spielen?
6. Er war schmutzig.
7. Sie kommen aus England.
8. Warum sitzen sie in der Küche?
9. Er stand in der Mitte des Zimmers.
10. Sie sieht tot aus.

2-3
1. Unser Gast
2. die Bücher
3. der Wagen
4. Das Kind
5. Die Musik
6. Meine Eltern
7. Das Glas
8. Der Berg
9. Angelika
10. Diese Diplomaten
11. sein Onkel
12. das Messer
13. Frau Bauer
14. Ihr Vetter
15. Ihre Kinder

Unit 3   Pronouns in the Accusative Case

3-1
1. Im Sommer werden wir sie besuchen.
2. Ich kenne es nicht.
3. Gudrun hat sie zu langsam beantwortet.
4. Kannst du sie lesen?
5. Wir haben ihn verpasst!
6. Wer kann es lösen?
7. Mutter hat ihn im Keller gefunden.
8. Der Blitz hat sie getötet.
9. Martin wird sie kaufen.
10. Ich liebe es.

3-2
These are sample answers only.
1. Ich habe den Herrn in Kanada kennen gelernt.
2. Wo hast du das Heft gefunden?
3. Er hat seine Brillen auf dem Tisch stehen gelassen.
4. Onkel Karl hat den Eimer versteckt.
5. Wirst du Karl und mich besuchen?
6. Man baut die Häuser am Rande des Waldes.
7. Tante Luise hat das Kind auf das Bett gelegt.

3-3
1. Was werde ich in Innsbruck verleben?
2. Wen kennt mein Vetter nicht?
3. Was kaufte Martin für seine Schwester?
4. Was hat sie seit ihrer Jugend getrieben?
5. Was verdient der Arbeitslose?
6. Wen treffen wir am Hauptbahnhof?
7. Wen hat meine Tante gefragt?
8. Was liebe ich am meisten?
9. Wen haben seine Eltern im Kaufhaus gesehen?
10. Wen ärgern solche Umstände?

3-4
1. es
2. ihn
3. sie
4. ihn
5. es
6. sie
7. euch
8. sie
9. ihn
10. ihn

Unit 4   Pronouns in the Dative Case

4-1
1. Er konnte ihm nicht antworten.
2. Ein Heft und Bleistifte nützen ihm.
3. Wir haben es ihm gegeben.
4. Ein kleines Segelboot hat sich ihr genähert.
5. Ich werde ihr ein paar Blumen kaufen.
6. Das wird ihnen nicht imponieren.
7. Martin schenkte es uns.
8. Der Hund ist ihr wieder entlaufen.
9. Kannst du ihnen helfen?
10. Der Professor schreibt ihm einen kurzen Brief.

4-2
1. a. Wer kann es mir erklären?
   b. Wer kann es dir erklären?
   c. Wer kann es uns erklären?
   d. Wer kann es euch erklären?
   e. Wer kann es Ihnen erklären?
2. a. Der Manager hat mir ein Telegramm geschickt.
   b. Der Manager hat dir ein Telegramm geschickt.
   c. Der Manager hat uns ein Telegramm geschickt.
   d. Der Manager hat euch ein Telegramm geschickt.
   e. Der Manager hat Ihnen ein Telegramm geschickt.
3. a. Was haben sie mir geschenkt?
   b. Was haben sie dir geschenkt?
   c. Was haben sie uns geschenkt?
   d. Was haben sie euch geschenkt?
   e. Was haben sie Ihnen geschenkt?

4-3
These are sample answers only.
1. Herr Schneider hat es dem jungen Rechtsanwalt gesagt.
2. Das hat den Wissenschaftlern sehr imponiert.
3. Was schenkst du deiner Tante?
4. Die Verkäuferin hat Karl und mir die neueste Mode gezeigt.
5. Angelika macht ihren Geschwistern eine kleine Überraschung.
6. Hat er dem Fremden geantwortet?
7. Zuerst müssen wir dem Kind die Jacke ausziehen.
8. Morgen geben wir es dem Arzt.

4-4
1. Wem habe ich geholfen?
2. Wem gehört dieses Fahrrad?
3. Wem hat es der Reiseleiter gezeigt?
4. Wem können wir nicht glauben?
5. Wem folgt er?
6. Wem kann ich es nicht geben?
7. Wem hat Tante Angelika eine neue Armbanduhr geschenkt?
8. Wem ist der Hund entlaufen?
9. Wem kann Martin helfen?
10. Wem wird er es schicken?

4-5
1. mir
2. es
3. ihnen
4. uns
5. ihr
6. mir
7. es
8. ihr
9. uns
10. ihnen

Unit 5   Pronouns in Prepositional Phrases

5-1

1. Ich habe für ihn gearbeitet.
2. Obwohl er schon 30 Jahre alt ist, wohnt er noch bei ihnen.
3. Wie lange müssen wir auf ihn warten?
4. Der Knabe hat sich immer vor ihm gefürchtet.
5. Die alte Frau sehnte sich nach ihr.
6. Ich habe ein paar Briefe von ihr bekommen.
7. Die tapferen Soldaten kämpfen gegen sie.
8. Es bestand ein großer Altersunterschied zwischen ihnen.
9. Die Touristen lachen über ihn.
10. Es ist fremdartig, dass Herr Keller ohne sie kommt.

5-2

1. a. Die Polizisten haben nach mir gerufen.
   b. Die Polizisten haben nach ihm gerufen.
   c. Die Polizisten haben nach Ihnen gerufen.
   d. Die Polizisten haben nach uns gerufen.
   e. Die Polizisten haben nach euch gerufen.
2. a. Warum spotten die Mädchen über dich?
   b. Warum spotten die Mädchen über sie?
   c. Warum spotten die Mädchen über sie?
   d. Warum spotten die Mädchen über ihn?
   e. Warum spotten die Mädchen über mich?
3. a. Oma sorgt sich immer um uns.
   b. Oma sorgt sich immer um mich.
   c. Oma sorgt sich immer um dich.
   d. Oma sorgt sich immer um sie.
   e. Oma sorgt sich immer um euch.

5-3

1. Für wen hat Karin ein Geschenk?
2. Von wem hat sie diese Gedichte bekommen?
3. Vor wem scheuten sich die Kinder?
4. Auf wen passt der Pförtner auf?
5. An wen hat Frau Gärtner oft gedacht?
6. Über wen haben wir die Nachricht geschickt?
7. Bei wem wohnte das junge Ehepaar?
8. Nach wem hat Ludwig gefragt?
9. Zu wem fährt der junge Mann?
10. Neben wen stellt sich das schüchterne Mädchen?

Unit 6 Direct and Indirect Object Pronouns in the Same Sentence

1. Sie haben ihm die neue Landkarte gezeigt.
2. Wirst du ihr eine Flasche Milch geben?
3. Er bringt ihr ein paar rote Nelken.
4. Ich habe es ihnen geschickt.
5. Marianne gab uns die alte Mundharmonika.
6. Er schenkte ihnen Ansichtskarten.
7. Sie verkauft ihm den alten VW.
8. Leiht er ihr das Fahrrad?
9. Wir teilten ihnen die neuesten Nachrichten mit.
10. Die Räuber raubten ihm die Geldtasche.

1. Frau Schneider reicht ihn dem Gast.
2. Meine Eltern haben sie dem Kellner bezahlt.
3. Der junge Mann wird ihn der alten Dame überlassen.
4. Können Sie ihn den Touristen zeigen?
5. Sie gibt es dem Zahnarzt.
6. Wirst du ihn deiner Frau schenken?
7. Ich kann es den Pferden geben.
8. Mutti wird es dem Kind ausziehen.
9. Wer schickte es Hans?
10. Der Taschendieb verweigerte sie dem Rechtsanwalt.

1. Ich reiche es ihm.
2. Doktor Schuhmann hat es ihm verboten.
3. Unsere Eltern haben sie uns geschenkt.
4. Die Kellnerin bringt sie ihnen.
5. Haben Sie sie ihr gegeben?

1. mir
2. dir
3. sie
4. uns
5. euch
6. ihnen
7. ihm
8. Ihnen
9. ihr
10. ihn

1. ihm
2. sie
3. Was
4. euch
5. ihr
6. sie
7. uns
8. es
9. ihn
10. mir

Unit 7   Possessive Pronouns

7-1
1. Kennst du seinen Bruder?
2. Seine Rede war ziemlich interessant.
3. Seine Stimme war so weich.
4. Ihr Schlafzimmer ist zu klein.
5. Ist seine Aktentasche noch im Büro?
6. Ihre Klassenzimmer sind im zweiten Stock.
7. Haben Sie sein Gebrüll gehört?
8. Ihr Spielzeug lag überall auf dem Fußboden.
9. Ich erkannte sofort sein Gesicht.
10. Wo ist ihr Schreibtisch?

7-2
1. Sie hat ihre neue Telefonnummer vergessen.
2. Wo hast du deinen Hund gefunden?
3. Ich steckte das Geld in meine Tasche.
4. Wir hängen unser Bild an die Wand.
5. Werdet ihr eure Verwandten in Bayern besuchen?
6. Wohnen Sie noch bei Ihren Freunden?
7. Haben sie ihrer Bekannten in Berlin geschrieben?
8. Sie sah ihren Hut aus dem Fenster des Autos verschwinden.
9. Wir haben das Rathaus unserer Stadt verbrennen sehen.
10. Ich habe meine Schwester nicht geschlagen.

7-3
1. Wessen Fahrrad ist gestern Nacht gestohlen worden?
2. Wessen Enkelkinder werden bald zu Besuch kommen?
3. Wessen Frage kann niemand beantworten?
4. Mit wessen Kusine hat Karl getanzt?
5. Auf wessen Schwestern werden wir nur noch ein paar Minuten warten?
6. Wessen Wecker ist zu laut?
7. Wessen Großvater haben sie versucht zu helfen?
8. Bei wessen Eltern will der Student wohnen?
9. Wessen ist zu klein?
10. Wessen Professor möchte Frau Schäfer kennen lernen?

7-4
These are sample answers only.
1. Wo ist denn mein Mantel?
2. Wir haben deinen Bekannten nicht erkannt.
3. Herr Bauer hat sein Geld nicht gefunden.
4. Die Kinder spielen mit ihren Freunden.
5. Kann niemand unserem Onkel helfen?
6. Ist Ihre Schwester krank?
7. Ich beschäftige mich mit meiner Aufgabe.
8. Angelika denkt an deinen Beruf.
9. Warum liest du nicht in deinem Buch?
10. Sie sieht ihren Freund.

Unit 8   *Einer/Keiner* and Interrogatives Used as Pronouns

8-1

1. a. Wir werden einen besuchen.
   b. Wir werden keinen besuchen.
2. a. Einer ist in der Kunsthalle geblieben. / Einige sind in der Kunsthalle geblieben.
   b. Keiner ist in der Kunsthalle geblieben. / Keine sind in der Kunsthalle geblieben.
3. a. Ich habe eine.
   b. Ich habe keine.
4. a. Hast du eines gekauft?
   b. Hast du keines gekauft?
5. a. Einer will nach Ägypten reisen. / Einige wollen nach Ägypten reisen.
   b. Keiner will nach Ägypten reisen. / Keine wollen nach Ägypten reisen.
6. a. Erhardt hat einen gekauft.
   b. Erhardt hat keinen gekauft.
7. a. Marianne spielt mit einer.
   b. Marianne spielt mit keiner.
8. a. Im Sommer trägt eine Dame eines.
   b. Im Sommer trägt eine Dame keines.
9. a. Eine betrifft meinen älteren Bruder.
   b. Keine betrifft meinen älteren Bruder.
10. a. Die kleinen Schüler gehorchten einem.
    b. Die kleinen Schüler gehorchten keinem.

8-2

1. Was haben die Jungen gegessen?
2. Wessen Pferd fütterte er?
3. Wen soll der alte Professor prüfen?
4. Mit wem hat der Reporter gesprochen?
5. Wen sahen die Mädchen dort spielen und schwimmen?
6. Was konnte das Kind nicht erreichen?
7. Wessen Eltern hat Klaudia vorgestellt?
8. Für wen hat Tante Luise ein Geschenk gekauft?

8-3

1. a. Welche Blumen hat ihr Johann geschenkt?
   b. Welche hat ihr Johann geschenkt?
2. a. Mit welcher Schauspielerin wollten sich die Theaterbesucher treffen?
   b. Mit welcher wollten sich die Theaterbesucher treffen?
3. a. Welches Schiff ist heute morgen von Bremerhaven abgefahren?
   b. Welches ist heute morgen von Bremerhaven abgefahren?
4. a. Welcher Obstbaum blüht jedes Jahr im April?
   b. Welcher blüht jedes Jahr im April?
5. a. In welche Scheune haben die Bauern das Korn gebracht?
   b. In welche haben die Bauern das Korn gebracht?
6. a. Welchen Wagen haben die alten Pferde gezogen?
   b. Welchen haben die alten Pferde gezogen?
7. a. Welche Kinder beobachtet die Lehrerin beim Spielen?
   b. Welche beobachtet die Lehrerin beim Spielen?
8. a. Welchen Besuchern hat der Fremdenführer das Museum gezeigt?
   b. Welchen hat der Fremdenführer das Museum gezeigt?
9. a. Wessen Kugel verwundete einen alten Herrn?
   b. Wessen verwundete einen alten Herrn?
10. a. Um welchen Namen hat er gebeten?
    b. Um welchen hat er gebeten?

Unit 9   Determiners Used as Pronouns

9-1
1. Kennst du diejenige Frau, die für Herrn Bauer gearbeitet hat?
2. Er sprach mit demjenigen Kind, das seine Mutter verloren hat.
3. Dasjenige Mädchen, von dem wir sprachen, ist eine Freundin von ihm.
4. Ich habe etwas für denjenigen Jungen, der weint.
5. Wir glauben denjenigen Leuten, die die fremdartige Geschichte erzählten.
6. Gerhardt hat denselben Schlips gekauft.
7. Hast du dir denselben Finger wieder gebrochen?
8. Hans kommt von derselben Stadt im Schwarzwald.
9. In demselben Irrgarten sind sie wieder verloren gegangen.
10. Ich möchte dasselbe.

9-2
1. Dieser kommt aus England.
2. Musst du dich in jeden verlieben?
3. Ich habe jenes in der Marktstraße gekauft.
4. Martin wollte diesen übersetzen.
5. Wir werden jedem schreiben.
6. Erich hat mit jener getanzt.

9-3
1. Ich würde niemals solchen kaufen.
2. Manche werden häufiger krank.
3. Ich habe mit vielen darüber gesprochen.
4. Welches willst du haben?
5. Das Theaterstück hat wenigen gefallen.
6. Alle wollen mit dem Meister Schach spielen.
7. Ich kenne nur einige hier.
8. Seine Zauberkraft hat mehreren imponiert.
9. Ich finde solche albern.
10. Wir werden alle in der Schweiz besuchen.

9-4
1. Ich habe etwas für euch.
2. Der arme Junge hat alles vergessen.
3. Martin kennt niemand im Hörsaal.
4. Jemand stand an der Ecke und weinte.
5. Warten Sie auf jemand?
6. Niemand lachte darüber.
7. Er hat alles verloren.
8. Wir werden jemand in Heidelberg treffen.
9. Haben Sie etwas gehört?
10. Der schüchterne Knabe will nichts singen.

9-5
These are sample answers only.
1. Wir werden jeden Gast besuchen wollen.
2. Sind alle Politiker wahnsinnig geworden?
3. Ich treffe diejenigen Kerle, die mich verspottet hatten.
4. Beide Jungen sind gute Freunde von mir.
5. Hast du ein Geschenk für mich?
6. Gudrun hat nur wenige Leute kennen gelernt.
7. Einige Ausländer wohnen noch im Harzgebirge.
8. Warum haben Sie solches Buch ausgewählt?
9. Kein Mensch versteht mich.
10. Meine Schwester möchte dieselbe Bluse haben.
11. Der neue Student konnte die Frage beantworten.
12. Welche Blusen haben Sie gekauft?
13. Diese Tassen sind viel besser.
14. Benno hat dasselbe Buch gefunden.
15. Werdet ihr beide Häuser verkaufen?

9-6

1. Die haben keine Ahnung!
2. Ich möchte mit dem sprechen.
3. Wir haben einen Brief von denen in Polen bekommen.
4. Angelika kommt mit der.
5. Die Katze schläft auf dem / darauf in der Ecke.

Unit 10   The Pronoun *man*

1. Wenn man sich nicht wohl fühlt, soll man zu Hause bleiben.
2. Was man kauft, das soll einem gefallen.
3. Hat man an der Ecke gewartet?
4. Man behauptet, dass er ein Taschendieb war.
5. Wie kann man etwas anderes erwarten?
6. Man soll dankbar sein, wenn einem auch ein kleines Geschenk gegeben wird.

1. Man hat es oft gesagt ...
2. Man betrug die alte Frau ...
3. Man wird sie davor warnen ...
4. Manchmal schreibt man ...
5. Man hofft ...

Unit 11 Relative Pronouns

1. a. Er findet einen Handschuh, der seinem Freund gehört.
   b. Er findet eine Mappe, die seinem Freund gehört.
   c. Er findet die Anzüge, die seinem Freund gehören.
2. a. Ich sprach mit einer Freundin, die Liese neulich kennen gelernt hat.
   b. Ich sprach mit dem Mädchen, das Liese neulich kennen gelernt hat.
   c. Ich sprach mit den Ausländern, die Liese neulich kennen gelernt hat.
3. a. Klaus kennt den Herrn, von dem die anderen gesprochen haben.
   b. Klaus kennt die Leute, von denen die anderen gesprochen haben.
   c. Klaus kennt das Kind, von dem die anderen gesprochen haben.
4. a. Sie besuchte ihre Verwandten, deren Nachbar aus England kommt.
   b. Sie besuchte den Professor, dessen Nachbar aus England kommt.
   c. Sie besuchte die Krankenschwester, deren Nachbar aus England kommt.

11-2

1. Der Tourist, mit welchem er gesprochen hat, war Ausländer.
2. Der Schriftsteller, dessen Romane viel bewundert werden, ist jetzt achtzig Jahre alt.
3. Sie haben Beethoven ein Denkmal gesetzt, welches ein junger Bildhauer geschaffen hat.
4. Sie kauft neue Gläser, aus welchen man nur Wein trinken wird.
5. Der Zug, welcher langsam fährt, ist kein Eilzug.

11-3

1. der
2. die
3. was
4. Wer
5. den
6. das
7. dem
8. dem
9. dessen
10. den

11-4

These are sample answers only.
1. ... die so hell leuchten.
2. ... was mir sehr gefiel.
3. ... er einen Artikel geschrieben hat.
4. ... der ihm gar nicht passt.
5. ... ich mich nicht interessiere.

Unit 12   Reflexive Pronouns

12-1

1. Ich möchte mich vorstellen.
2. Wir haben uns wieder geärgert.
3. Du musst dich vor einer Erkältung schützen.
4. Habt ihr euch angekleidet?
5. Wie können sie sich ändern?
6. Meine Mutter fragt sich, was geschehen ist.
7. Frau Schneider hat sich auf einen Stuhl gesetzt.
8. Du hast dich schon überzeugt.
9. Der wahnsinnige Mann hat sich getötet.
10. Ich wasche mich.

12-2

1. Die Mutter putzt sich die Zähne.
2. Gudrun hilft sich, so gut sie kann.
3. Martin und Erich wollen sich ein Spiel kaufen.
4. Warum musst du dir widersprechen?
5. Ich kämme mir die Haare.
6. Darf ich mir ein Stück Kuchen nehmen?
7. Meine Schwester hat sich ein interessantes Buch gefunden.
8. Er kaufte sich eine Armbanduhr.
9. Das wird sie sich nie verzeihen.
10. Habt ihr euch die Mäntel ausgezogen?

12-3

1. Was hat sich bewegt?
2. Ich kann mir nicht helfen.
3. Haben Sie sich nicht widersprochen?
4. Wir haben uns vorgestellt.
5. Wer hat sich gewaschen?
6. Sie hat sich an die Italienreise erinnert.
7. Man soll sich nicht ärgern.
8. Herr Finkler hat sich einen neuen Wagen gekauft.
9. Sie haben sich ein paar Pralinen genommen.
10. Du musst dich ändern.

12-4

1. a. Ich denke nur an mich.
   b. Du denkst nur an dich.
   c. Die Kinder denken nur an sich.
   d. Sie denken nur an sich.
2. a. Ich kaufte mir neue Handschuhe.
   b. Er kaufte sich neue Handschuhe.
   c. Wir kauften uns neue Handschuhe.
   d. Du kauftest dir neue Handschuhe.
3. a. Der alte Mann braucht Hustentropfen für sich.
   b. Sie braucht Hustentropfen für sich.
   c. Ihr braucht Hustentropfen für euch.
   d. Erich braucht Hustentropfen für sich.

12-5

These are sample answers only.
1. Wir werden dem neuen Angestellten diese Arbeit zutrauen.
2. Braucht ihr das Geld für euren Onkel?
3. Ich kann meinen Chef nicht davon überzeugen.
4. Sie dürfen das Kind auf diese Bank setzen.
5. Marianne stellte die Stehlampe neben ihren Vater.
6. Meine Eltern haben einem Freund einen bunten Teppich gekauft.
7. Er fragt Gudrun, ob das eine Dummheit ist.
8. Du sollst deine Eltern sofort vorstellen.
9. Karl hat seiner Freundin einen guten Platz gesucht.
10. Ich ziehe dem Kind das Hemd an.

12-6

1. mich
2. dich
3. sich
4. sich
5. euch
6. sich
7. sich
8. mir
9. dich
10. mir

Unit 13   Reciprocal Pronouns

13-1

1. Erich und Klaus schicken einander ein paar Briefe.
2. Die Ausländer verstehen einander nicht.
3. Die Schwestern kauften einander Geschenke.
4. Die Reisenden wollten miteinander sprechen.
5. Wir besuchten einander.
6. Die Tennisspieler spielen sehr schlecht gegeneinander.
7. Die Jungen und Mädchen beobachten einander.
8. Oma und Opa sorgen umeinander.
9. Karl und Klaudia haben nacheinander gefragt.
10. Er stellt die Vasen nebeneinander.

13-2

These are sample answers only.
1. Können sie einander sehen?
2. Sie haben sich lange miteinander unterhalten.
3. Oft arbeiten sie füreinander.
4. Warum habt ihr gegeneinander gesprochen?
5. Sie reden voneinander.

PART II Prepositions
Unit 14 Accusative Prepositions

14-1

1. a. Eine Fledermaus ist durch das Haus geflogen.
   b. Eine Fledermaus ist durch die Scheune geflogen.
   c. Eine Fledermaus ist durch den großen Lesesaal geflogen.
   d. Eine Fledermaus ist durch unsere Schule geflogen.
2. a. Warum ist er gegen seine Kinder?
   b. Warum ist er gegen seinen Sohn?
   c. Warum ist er gegen ihren älteren Bruder?
   d. Warum ist er gegen seine Tante?
3. a. Der neue Manager handelte ohne jede Rücksicht auf uns.
   b. Der neue Manager handelte ohne Vernunft.
   c. Der neue Manager handelte ohne Überlegung.
4. a. Ich möchte bis Freitag bleiben.
   b. Ich möchte bis nächsten Samstag bleiben.
   c. Ich möchte bis morgen bleiben.
5. a. Welcher Weg führt den schönen Bach entlang?
   b. Welcher Weg führt diesen Wald entlang?
   c. Welcher Weg führt jenen Zaun entlang?
   d. Welcher Weg führt keinen Fluss entlang?

14-2

1. um
2. bis
3. um
4. für
5. für
6. für
7. um
8. bis
9. um (bis)
10. um

14-3

These are sample answers only.
1. meine Familie
2. die Wand
3. zwanzig Uhr
4. halb elf
5. einen breiten Fluss
6. Heidelberg
7. der Stadtmauer
8. seinen Regenschirm
9. meine Enkelkinder
10. den Bach
11. meinen Pass
12. ein Gewitter
13. Hilfe
14. die neuen Schüler
15. mich

Unit 15   Dative Prepositions

15-1

1. a. Eine Fledermaus ist aus dem Haus geflogen.
   b. Eine Fledermaus ist aus der Kirche geflogen.
   c. Eine Fledermaus ist aus einem großen Fenster geflogen.
   d. Eine Fledermaus ist aus diesem Tunnel geflogen.
2. a. Wie lange wirst du bei deiner Tante wohnen?
   b. Wie lange wirst du bei diesen Leuten wohnen?
   c. Wie lange wirst du bei einem Bekannten wohnen?
   d. Wie lange wirst du bei deinem Onkel wohnen?
3. a. Wir sind sehr zufrieden mit Ihrer Arbeit.
   b. Wir sind sehr zufrieden mit dieser Lösung.
   c. Wir sind sehr zufrieden mit einigen Theorien.
   d. Wir sind sehr zufrieden mit dem neuen Angestellten.
4. a. Karl ist sehr unterschiedlich von seinem Vater.
   b. Karl ist sehr unterschiedlich von seinen Geschwistern.
   c. Karl ist sehr unterschiedlich von seiner Schwester.
   d. Karl ist sehr unterschiedlich von seinen Eltern.

15-2

1. nach
2. zu
3. von
4. zu
5. zu/von
6. aus
7. von
8. zu
9. aus/zu
10. aus
11. nach
12. Nach
13. zu
14. von
15. von

15-3

These are sample answers only.
1. dem Krieg
2. April
3. meiner Tante
4. dem jungen Reporter
5. der Gaststätte
6. persönlicher Erfahrung
7. dem Hauptmann
8. seinen Freunden
9. dem Film
10. Dem Eingang
11. Berlin
12. zwei Kollegen
13. ersten
14. dem Bus
15. Eiche

Unit 16   Accusative-Dative Prepositions

16-1

1. a. Eine Fledermaus ist zwischen die Häuser geflogen.
   b. Eine Fledermaus ist zwischen die Kirche und die Schule geflogen.
   c. Eine Fledermaus ist zwischen einen Turm und ein Haus.
2. a. Wer sitzt neben deinem Bruder?
   b. Wer sitzt neben ihm?
   c. Wer sitzt neben Ihrer Tante?
   d. Wer sitzt neben den kleinen Fenstern?
3. a. Der bellende Hund läuft an die Tür.
   b. Der bellende Hund läuft an das offene Fenster.
   c. Der bellende Hund läuft an den großen Spiegel.
4. a. Kleiner Benno versteckte sich hinter einem großen Baum.
   b. Kleiner Benno versteckte sich hinter dem Schrank.
   c. Kleiner Benno versteckte sich hinter den blauen Gardinen.
   d. Kleiner Benno versteckte sich hinter einer Mauer.

16-2

1. in
2. auf
3. hinter/unter
4. auf
5. auf
6. unter
7. in
8. in
9. hinter
10. auf

16-3

These are sample answers only.
1. meine Kindheit
2. der Wand
3. dem Bauernhof
4. deine Tasche
5. den Berg
6. der Universität
7. deutsch
8. dem Schrank
9. dem Bett und dem Stuhl
10. dem Turm
11. vierzig Jahren alt
12. der Kirche
13. Helga
14. dem Spazierweg
15. seine Ankunft

16-4

1. in
2. an
3. hinter
4. an
5. auf
6. auf
7. über
8. vor
9. auf
10. zwischen

Unit 17   Genitive Prepositions

17-1

1. a. Ich kann wegen des Gewitters leider nicht kommen.
   b. Ich kann wegen einer Erkältung leider nicht kommen.
   c. Ich kann wegen seines Todes leider nicht kommen.
2. a. Während der Ferien waren wir am Bodensee.
   b. Während unseres Urlaubs waren wir am Bodensee.
   c. Während der wärmsten Tage waren wir am Bodensee.
3. a. Eine enge Straße führte oberhalb des kleinen Rathauses.
   b. Eine enge Straße führte oberhalb eines schönen Parks.
   c. Eine enge Straße führte oberhalb der Gaststätte.
4. a. Trotz des Wetters geht mein Großvater täglich zur Arbeit.
   b. Trotz seines hohen Alters geht mein Großvater täglich zur Arbeit.
   c. Trotz der furchtbaren Kälte geht mein Großvater täglich zur Arbeit.
5. a. Statt eines Pfarrers ist ein junger Arzt gekommen.
   b. Statt seiner Verwandten ist ein junger Arzt gekommen.
   c. Statt einer Krankenschwester ist ein junger Arzt gekommen.

17-2

1. diesseits
2. Anstatt
3. Während
4. wegen
5. Anstatt
6. Während
7. Diesseits
8. wegen
9. während
10. Anstatt

17-3

These are sample answers only.
1. der Festung
2. des Berges
3. seines kahlen Kopfes
4. eines Unfalls / einem Unfall
5. des Flusses
6. des Winters
7. der kleinen Stadt
8. des Mittelmeers
9. des Dorfes
10. einer Tasse Tee
11. des Familienkreises
12. einer langen Krankheit
13. des Sommers
14. des Gewitters
15. eines neuen Wagens

Unit 18   Prepositional Adverbs

 18-1

1. davor, wovor
2. dabei, wobei
3. darin, worin
4. darauf, worauf
5. damit, womit
6. dazu, wozu
7. daran, woran
8. daraus, woraus
9. daneben, woneben
10. dadurch, wodurch
11. danach, wonach
12. dafür, wofür
13. dagegen, wogegen
14. darum, worum
15. darüber, worüber

18-2

1. Haben Sie mehr als 200 Euro dafür gezahlt?
2. Ich habe mich sehr darüber gefreut.
3. Man muss dagegen kämpfen.
4. Der Graf herrschte darüber.
5. Er fürchtet sich davor.
6. Gudrun denkt oft daran.
7. Was wollen Sie damit?
8. Erich hat noch nichts davon gehört.
9. Herr Schneider hat dafür gesorgt.
10. Mein älterer Bruder hat mir damit geholfen.

18-3

1. Wofür interessieren sie sich?
2. Wonach riefen die armen Bürger?
3. Woran habe ich oft gedacht?
4. Worauf hoffen die Eltern?
5. Womit spielt ein kleiner Knabe?
6. Wofür ist seine Eifersucht ein Beweis?
7. Worauf freute ich mich sehr?
8. Wonach fragte der Arzt?
9. Woran lief die neugierige Katze?
10. Wovor fürchtet er sich?

18-4

These are sample answers only.
1. Ich habe mich sehr auf die Party gefreut.
2. Was macht ihr mit diesen Sachen?
3. Sie denkt wieder an seinen Tod.
4. Karl wird nach ihrer Gesundheit fragen.
5. Interessierst du dich für klassische Musik?
6. Ich warte auf die Straßenbahn.
7. Ich freue mich über diesen Brief.
8. Er hat sich an seine Heimat erinnert.
9. Sie schützen sich gegen den kalten Wind.
10. Die Eltern sorgen für das Essen.

Unit 19   Verbs with a Prepositional Object

1. an, to take part in
2. um, to ask for
3. nach, to ask about
4. bei, to live at someone's house
5. vor, to be afraid of
6. auf, to watch out for
7. um, to apply for
8. von, to depend on
9. mit, to stop (with)
10. über, to speak about
11. bei, to thank
12. aus, to be from / made out of
13. aus, to come from
14. an, to believe in
15. gegen, to struggle against

19-2

1. a. Du sollst die Touristen vor dieser Gefahr warnen.
   b. Du sollst die Touristen vor den Untersuchungen warnen.
   c. Du sollst die Touristen vor dem Taschendieb warnen.
2. a. Ich kann mich immer auf meinen Vater verlassen.
   b. Ich kann mich immer auf die junge Ärztin verlassen.
   c. Ich kann mich immer auf seine Vernunft verlassen.
3. a. Wenn er einsam ist, denkt er an seine Heimat.
   b. Wenn er einsam ist, denkt er an einen guten Freund in Berlin.
   c. Wenn er einsam ist, denkt er an sie.
4. a. Erzählen Sie bitte von Ihrer Vergangenheit!
   b. Erzählen Sie bitte von dem Leben in Amerika!
   c. Erzählen Sie bitte von Ihren Reisen!

19-3

These are sample answers only.
1. euch
2. Berlin
3. meine Frage
4. die Physik
5. einem neuen Freund
6. das Geld
7. das Essen
8. einem Sportverein
9. meinen Ausweis
10. dem Zug

19-4

1. an
2. auf
3. bei
4. mit
5. über
6. aus
7. für
8. nach
9. an
10. mit

Unit 20 Adjectives with a Prepositional Object

20-1

1. in, in love with
2. zu, ready for
3. an, poor in
4. an, rich in
5. mit, satisfied with
6. zu, kind to
7. auf, attentive to
8. mit, acquainted with
9. von, different from
10. auf, angry at (with)
11. zu, capable of
12. von, convinced of
13. auf, jealous of
14. auf, proud of
15. über, happy about

20-2

1. a. Ist Gudrun zufrieden mit ihrem Aufsatz?
   b. Ist Gudrun zufrieden mit ihrer Brille?
   c. Ist Gudrun zufrieden mit ihren neuen Schuhen?
2. a. Der Lehrer war sehr böse auf die ganze Klasse.
   b. Der Lehrer war sehr böse auf den faulen Schüler.
   c. Der Lehrer war sehr böse auf diese Jungen.
3. a. Ich bin noch nicht von deiner Theorie überzeugt.
   b. Ich bin noch nicht von Ihren Ideen überzeugt.
   c. Ich bin noch nicht von diesem Plan überzeugt.
4. a. Der Richter ist mit vielen Politikern bekannt.
   b. Der Richter ist mit dem Bürgermeister bekannt.
   c. Der Richter ist mit meiner jüngsten Tochter bekannt.
5. a. Frau Keller ist sehr stolz auf ihre Kinder.
   b. Frau Keller ist sehr stolz auf diese Studentin.
   c. Frau Keller ist sehr stolz auf unseren Fortschritt.

20-3

These are sample answers only.

1. lesen
2. mich
3. diese Knaben
4. seiner Hausarbeit
5. die Frau seines Bruders
6. uns
7. meiner Erziehung
8. seine Soldaten
9. dem neuen Lehrer
10. Kohle

20-4

1. an
2. in
3. zu
4. über
5. mit
6. auf
7. auf
8. für
9. auf
10. von

Unit 21   Prepositions as Prefixes

1. **Über**mensch
2. **hinter**gehen
3. **bis**her
4. **Durch**bruch
5. **für**sprechen
6. **vor**ehelich
7. **unter**bewusst
8. **Auf**zug
9. **unter**brechen
10. **über**natürlich
11. **Neben**frage
12. **ein**förmig
13. **Ein**gang
14. **an**einander
15. **Zwischen**station

21-2

1. **durch**reisen, to travel through
2. **auf**hören, to stop
3. **mit**singen, to sing along
4. **durch**lesen, to read through
5. **an**kommen, to arrive
6. **durch**fahren, to drive through
7. **mit**fliegen, to fly along
8. **Unter**schrift, signature
9. **aus**trinken, to finish drinking
10. **Aus**sicht, view

Unit 22 Prepositional Contractions

22-1

1. X
2. aufs
3. ans
4. zum
5. zur
6. X
7. fürs
8. im
9. ums
10. X
11. ins
12. beim
13. vom
14. X
15. X

22-2

These are sample answers only.
1. Ihre Tante sitzt im Wohnzimmer.
2. Die Jungen laufen ins Haus.
3. Vater ist eben vom Bahnhof gekommen.
4. Fahrt ihr jetzt aufs Land?
5. Wie kommt man zum Rathaus?
6. Ist das der Weg zur Bibliothek?
7. Er bat mich ums Brot.
8. Jemand steht am Fenster.
9. Die Ritter laufen ans Tor.
10. Der alte Mann wohnte beim Enkelkind.

Review Exercises

R-1

1. Ich 2. Wir 3. du 4. ihr 5. Sie 6. Sie 7. Sie 8. Sie 9. Ich 10. Er 11. Es 12. ihr 13. es 14. er 15. Sie

R-2

1. b 2. a 3. a 4. d 5. b 6. d 7. a 8. a 9. a 10. d

R-3

1. schläft 2. Ist 3. haben 4. spielen 5. nimmt 6. wird 7. Kannst 8. muss 9. Wollt 10. spricht

R-4

1. ihn 2. es 3. sie 4. ihn 5. es 6. ihn 7. sie 8. sie 9. es 10. ihn 11. uns 12. sie 13. es 14. sie 15. sie

R-5

1. c 2. b 3. c 4. a 5. b 6. b 7. a 8. d 9. c 10. d

R-6

1. ohne sie 2. um es 3. dafür 4. darum 5. ohne ihn 6. dadurch 7. ohne sie 8. dagegen 9. für ihn 10. dadurch

R-7

1. ihr 2. mit ihr 3. ihnen 4. zu ihnen 5. daraus 6. ihr 7. ihm 8. danach 9. bei ihr 10. ihm 11. ihnen 12. von ihr 13. ihnen 14. mit uns 15. davon

R-8

1. ihm 2. ihn 3. ihr 4. es 5. er 6. ihm 7. sie 8. ihn 9. Er 10. es 11. ihr 12. ihnen 13. ihm 14. ihm 15. Es

R-9

1. mein 2. dein 3. sein 4. ihr 5. sein 6. unser 7. euer 8. ihr 9. Ihr 10. wessen

R-10

1. mir 2. euch 3. sich 4. sich 5. sich 6. sich 7. uns 8. dich 9. sich 10. dir

R-11

1. seine Kinder, ihren älteren Bruder
2. jede Rücksicht auf uns, Vernunft
3. Montag, nächste Woche
4. meine Familie, meinen Sohn
5. das Haus, den großen Lesesaal

R-12

1. um 2. bis 3. für 4. für 5. um

R-13

1. meiner Mutter, unseren Kindern
2. Ihrer Tante, einem Bekannten
3. diesem Zimmer, dem neuen Manager
4. seinem Vater, seinen Brüdern
5. ihm, Ihnen

R-14

1. die Häuser 2. ihm 3. das offene Fenster 4. den Boden 5. der Tür 6. einem Vorort 7. dem Dach 8. jenem Tisch 9. fünf Minuten 10. den Schrank

R-15

1. eines Gewitters, eines Schneesturms
2. ihrer Ohrringe, meiner Brille
3. seiner Krankheit, des Unfalls
4. unserer Kinder, unseres Problems
5. des Flusses, der Berge
6. seiner Familie, der Partei
7. des ganzen Tages, der ersten zwei Stunden
8. eines Geschenks, eines langen Briefes
9. einer Erkältung, des Todes meiner Großmutter
10. des Krieges, seiner Warnung

R-16   1. a 2. d 3. b 4. c 5. a 6. c 7. c 8. d 9. a 10. b 11. a 12. d 13. a 14. a 15. c

R-17   1. soll 2. ihn 3. kommst 4. dich 5. Welchen 6. sie 7. für 8. unseren 9. mir 10. seinen
11. du 12. bestellt/bestellte; bestellen/bestellten 13. ihm 14. Ihnen 15. hat 16. zwischen
17. außer 18. es 19. des Schnees 20. dem Klavier/einem Klavier 21. Ihr 22. mich 23. der
Hauptstraße 24. Es 25. um 26. Welches 27. zwei 28. dem neuen Anzug 29. auf 30. was
31. nebeneinander 32. Wer 33. meines 34. dich 35. an